Learning for Success

THIRD EDITION

Learning for Success

EFFECTIVE STRATEGIES FOR STUDENTS

Joan Fleet

Fiona Goodchild

Richard Zajchowski

Advising & Career Centre
Room S302
U of T @ Scarborough

HARCOURT
BRACE
CANADA

Harcourt Brace & Company, Canada

Toronto Montreal Fort Worth New York Orlando
Philadelphia San Diego London Sydney Tokyo

Canadian Cataloguing in Publication Data

Fleet, Joan, 1939–
    Learning for success

3rd ed.
Previously published under title: Learning for success : skills and strategies for Canadian students.
ISBN 0-7747-3659-3

1. Study Skills.   I. Goodchild, Fiona, 1943– .   II. Zajchowski, Richard.   III. Title.

LB1049.F48 1999   378.1'7028'1   C98-932207-6

New Editions Editor: Liz Radojkovic
Production Editor: Carolyn McLarty
Senior Production Co-ordinator: Sue-Ann Becker

Copy Editor: Focus Strategic Communications
Photo Researcher: Jeannine Maxfield
Cover Design: Sonya V. Thursby, Opus House Incorporated, Sharon Foster Design
Interior Design: Sharon Foster Design
Cover Photo: Dick Hemingway
Typesetting and Assembly: Sharon Foster Design
Printing and Binding: Kromar Printing

Harcourt Brace & Company Canada, Ltd.
55 Horner Avenue, Toronto, ON, Canada M8Z 4X6
Customer Service
Toll-Free Tel.: 1-800-387-7278
Toll-Free Fax: 1-800-665-7307

This book was printed in Canada.

1 2 3 4 5   03 02 01 00 99

Contents

Chapter 6   Learning from Lectures   78

Chapter 7   Learning from Textbooks   93

Chapter 8 Problem Solving in Science and Engineering 114

Chapter 9 Preparing for Exams 135

PART 4 EFFECTIVE APPLICATION OF KNOWLEDGE 149

Chapter 10 Writing Exams 151

Preface

Learning for Success: Effective Strategies for Students, Third Edition, was written for college and university students as well as for high-school students planning to go on to post-secondary education. It is specifically for students who are seeking new and more effective ways to be successful academically. The unifying theme of this book is that successful students are strategic learners. Strategies for academic tasks are presented, and students are invited to think about and select those that will work best for their own situation. The many worksheets in this book are an important tool for developing a personal approach to learning.

This third edition retains much of what students have told us they have found useful in the previous two editions. In addition, we have brought the content up to date in the light of changes in education, specifically the widespread use of computers by students. We have also included suggestions from readers, and we have made revisions to clarify and expand upon concepts and strategies. Finally, we have given the book a whole new look that we hope you will find attractive and will make your reading easier.

WELCOME TO STUDENTS READING THIS BOOK

There are four main goals for this book:

1. To increase your awareness of yourself as a learner.
2. To suggest that you can control many of the factors affecting your own successful academic performance.
3. To introduce specific skills for more effective learning.
4. To help you to incorporate new and more effective learning strategies into your own personal approach to learning.

Facing the Learning Challenge

Most students are natural learners in that they do not give much thought to the way in which they learn. They just do it, and many do it quite well. You may be such a student, and you may have found that your approach to learning has generally lead to academic success. However, there may also have been times when things did not go so well: for example, when you took a new course or had to adjust to a teacher with a different teaching style. You may also have experienced difficulty with transitions to a higher grade or moving from one school to another. It probably seemed like moving up to the big leagues—everything was faster and more challenging.

New academic experiences, however, can be a time for great personal growth for you, especially if you are willing to invest time in developing your learning strategies. The four goals of this book are all directed to helping you adjust to new learning experiences and, consequently, helping you to grow as a learner. In each chapter, you will find many suggested learning strategies to help you reach your academic goals. Some of these will not be new to you. As a learner, you have already acquired study patterns, and you will want to retain and strengthen those that currently work well for you. However, we hope that you will find many new ideas in this book that you will consider trying.

No two students are exactly alike in the way they study, and so selected strategies vary from person to person. As you read this book, choose those strategies that you think may be useful to you, but remember to give them time to work. It takes a certain amount of effort to change your current approach and to develop new and effective study strategies.

An important first step in developing new study strategies is to be aware of the way you learn currently. You will want to build on your strengths as a learner as well as work on areas in which you are weak. The following self-assessment covers some of the important decisions that you need to make to be a successful learner.

ASSESSING YOUR STUDY STRATEGIES

For each item, check either YES (this is often or usually typical of me) or NO (this is seldom or never typical of me).

A. Immediate Study Environment

Do you:

	Yes	No
1. Select a study location relatively free from distractions?	___	___
2. Select a study location with adequate light and ventilation?	___	___
3. Have ready access to a computer and the Internet?	___	___
4. Have on hand materials you will need: paper, stapler, calculator?	___	___
5. Have a calendar visible with all key dates clearly shown?	___	___
6. Set up a system to organize all notes and handouts for each course so that you can quickly locate essential materials such as old tests?	___	___
7. Plan your time so that you can devote a reasonable amount to each course?	___	___

B. Campus Resources

Have you found:

	Yes	No
1. Other students who are willing to be part of a study group for each course you are taking?	___	___
2. When and what kind of help is available from your instructor or tutor?	___	___
3. The help centres for your courses?	___	___
4. Ways of preparing questions so that your times with a resource person are as useful as possible?	___	___
5. Where old exams are available (e.g., library) and how to get them?	___	___
6. Any alternate textbooks and reference material that may be helpful?	___	___
7. The location of important bulletin boards displaying key information (e.g., solutions to selected problems)?	___	___
8. Where and what kind of assistance is available at the counselling centre, health services, and other student services?	___	___

C. Personal Health and Effectiveness

Do you maintain:

<table>
<tr><td></td><td>Yes</td><td>No</td></tr>
</table>

1. A regular sleep pattern (seven to nine hours per night)?
2. A study plan that sets aside regular and sufficient hours for study?
3. A daily balanced diet?
4. A reasonable amount of regular exercise?
5. A drug- and alcohol-free lifestyle?

Do you make time for:

6. A few hours a week for your own enjoyment?
7. Getting away for a while, either physically or mentally, when problems or pressures arise?
8. Finding and talking to people to whom you can turn when you encounter difficulties?
9. Practising relaxation techniques so that you can calm down if necessary?
10. Socializing with other students who want to do well at school?
11. Focussing on the needs of others around you?

D. Academic Thinking Skills

Do you consciously plan to:

<table>
<tr><td></td><td>Yes</td><td>No</td></tr>
</table>

1. Reduce information by listening and reading for key ideas?
2. Keep track of the overall structure of the information by tracking themes using headings?
3. Repeat silently to yourself information that you are recording so that you won't forget it before writing it down?
4. Identify possible test questions from lectures and readings?
5. Self-test by answering questions from memory or by writing out important concepts from memory?
6. Use a variety of methods to develop a good memory of the content?
7. Keep track of the stated aims and objectives of the course (e.g., by periodically reading the course outline and listening for messages from the instructor)?
8. Review regularly to avoid forgetting?

As you review your answers to the questions on the previous two pages, can you identify areas of strength that contribute to your academic success? Can you also identify weaknesses in your learning techniques that you wish to review and change? This self-awareness is necessary if you want to find the best approach to your studies.

My Current Strengths

_____

_____

_____

My Current Weaknesses

_____

_____

_____

PART 1

An Introduction to Strategic Learning

CHAPTER 1

The Good Strategy User

LEARNING OBJECTIVES

The purpose of this chapter is for you to:

➜ Read about the unifying theme of this book—the Good Strategy User.
➜ Recognize that adequate background knowledge is essential for academic success.
➜ Think about the roles of your attitudes and beliefs about learning.
➜ Explore two types of strategies: self-management and thinking strategies.
➜ Rate yourself as a Good Strategy User.

WHEN PEOPLE USED to talk about a student's progress, they often used terms such as bright, average, or poor. These days, however, we realize how complex learning is, and we no longer try to explain a student's progress with such simplistic terms. Although natural ability is an important component of academic success, other factors such as home background and experiences, personality, formal schooling, motivation, and persistence can also contribute. In addition, successful students, regardless of any other factors, typically apply effective learning strategies to their tasks. While students may not have been able to control all the factors that have affected their past academic progress, they can take charge of the current learning strategies that they choose to apply.

The focus of this book, therefore, is on learning strategies. It assumes that since your goal in reading this book is to be a successful student, you will make conscious choices about how you study. In other words, you will take a strategic approach to learning. Thinking about the academic challenges that face you and making strategic choices can be made easier if you have a system for organizing your thinking about your own learning approach and strategy use. The Good Strategy User model[1] introduced in this chapter and used throughout this book provides you with such a structured starting place. This model presents four components for you to consider when making academic choices: your background knowledge, your attitudes and beliefs, two types of strategies that you apply, and your ability to take control and make any necessary changes to your current approach.

THE SUCCESSFUL LEARNER

Melanie is a first-year student who has just received a test result in her introductory history course. She can't wait to get back to residence to share the great news with her room-mate Karen that her very first test mark is an A.

---

[1] The term "Good Strategy User" was first used in Pressley, M., Borkowski, J.G., & Schneider, W. (1987). Cognitive strategies: Good strategy users coordinate metacognition and knowledge. *Annals of Child Development, 4*, 89–129.

Karen responds just as Melanie expects with a wild yell, and she dances around the room. Then she flops on the bed and says, "You know, I'm not at all surprised that you got that A because..."

1. _____

_____

_____

2. _____

_____

_____

3. _____

_____

_____

How do you think that Karen is explaining Melanie's success? Can you fill in some of the reasons why Melanie's mark was an A? Try to list at least three reasons before reading further.

THE GOOD STRATEGY USER

One explanation that modern educators might give for Melanie's A is that she is a Good Strategy User. This idea contrasts with the more traditional view that the two main reasons for Melanie's A are that Melanie has a high IQ and that she works hard. While these are important, there is a lot of evidence to suggest that performance in school can be greatly enhanced through the appropriate use of learned strategies. Success is not simply a matter of innate ability and hours upon hours of study.

Let us take a closer look at four components that contribute to effective use of strategies in Melanie's case: her background knowledge, her personal attitudes to and beliefs about school, her learning strategies, and her strategic awareness. As you read, think about your own academic performance. How does each one of these four components contribute to your success?

Background Knowledge

Melanie took history every year in high school, so this introductory course does not contain too many surprises. For example, the struggles between the French and English settlers in Canada are not new to her, although never before has she gone into such a detailed analysis of the Acadian deportation. Her previous history courses have provided Melanie with an adequate background, so she seldom feels overwhelmed or lost in class. In addition, she prepares for each class by reading ahead in the text. She knows that she gets a lot more out of a lecture when she has done her homework thoroughly and has a sound knowledge base of the current topic.

If you are to be a Good Strategy User, you need a knowledge base that is at least minimally adequate for a course. You may not always be able to select courses for which you have a very extensive base of knowledge, but your level of knowledge should be such that you are not constantly struggling to keep your head above water. An inadequate knowledge base in one course can lead to an overly demanding workload, which can sabotage your efforts in other courses by leaving inadequate time for you to study.

In addition to the general knowledge that you bring to a course, the specific background knowledge that you gain by preparing for each class is also critical to your successful performance. Completing assigned readings allows for greater class participation by letting you listen and record more effectively and contribute to class discussion.

Personal Attitudes and Beliefs

Melanie enjoys being a student. At this stage in her life, school is where she wants to be. Although she does find some things difficult, she believes that she can do well if she plans her activities and chooses appropriate strategies to meet important goals. She wants a balanced life as a student. She does not feel guilty taking time out to play squash, knowing that she has planned for that, because she is a firm believer in both working and playing hard. She is prepared to give her studies her best shot, and right now things are looking good.

Attitudes

A positive attitude—to being a student, to school, to classmates, to courses and programs—is a major contributor to success. A positive attitude translates into enthusiasm and energy to do work, and with it you are more likely to take a thoughtful, strategic approach to studying. As soon as you tell yourself that you do not like being in school or that you do not like a specific course, you have made your situation much more difficult. If you can find ways to make your courses enjoyable even when faced with some difficulties, it is much more likely that you will succeed.

Beliefs

Beliefs that you hold about various aspects of school can have a major influence on your use of study strategies. For example, if you believe that multiple-choice tests are out to trick you or that math problems are meant to be difficult, then you will be much less likely to put in any real effort and will be less likely to improve and succeed in these areas. Beliefs can be resistant to change because they have often developed over a long period of time. It is important to evaluate beliefs that you hold about your potential to succeed and to work on any that you feel are blocking your progress.

Learning Strategies

Reading the text before class is one specific strategy that works for Melanie. Applying such learning strategies to tasks is crucial to good strategy use. Unfortunately, many students confuse general good intentions (working harder or managing time better) with strategies. Good intentions rarely translate into effective action unless they are rephrased as specific strategies. As a Good Strategy User, Melanie sets important goals, plans the steps to reach those goals, and then translates the steps into specific strategies that she puts into action. By being strategic, Melanie accomplishes her study task goals in the most optimal ways possible.

It is useful to recognize two major types of strategies, both of which are essential to academic success. One set, the self-management strategies, enable Melanie to control her learning environment. The second set, the academic-thinking strategies, engage Melanie's thinking skills and are applied by her as she processes the course content.

Self-Management Strategies

Melanie manages the environment in which she studies.

- She has a favourite quiet corner in the library, and she always goes there to read the history text.
- She sits where the lighting is just right so that her eyes do not get tired.
- She sets a goal of reading ten pages before taking a short break.

Self-management strategies that set the environment for study are the first steps to accomplishing learning goals. For a given academic goal, you will need to decide where you will study. Some students prefer a very quiet and undisturbed location, while others concentrate better in more social settings. It is a good idea to vary your work location depending on your needs. At times, your study location may be dictated by necessary technological supports such as a computer or lab equipment. A library, classroom, lounge, or your own room can all be good places to study.

Keep in mind factors such as lighting, comfort and convenience of the furniture, ventilation, and potential distractions. Plan to have all necessary materials at hand, especially if you are working away from your own room. For optimum concentration, schedule your meals so that you are not hungry or too full as you study. Think carefully about what you will wear as you do not want to be physically uncomfortable while you study.

You will need to consider the best times to accomplish certain tasks. For example, it may suit you best to work on math problems in the morning and read your novels for your Canadian literature course in the evening. The Good Strategy User is aware of the best times for academic tasks. Strategic use of resources also affects the quality of your learning environment. In addition to consultations with your instructors, there may be other important resources available such as writing and counselling centres and computer facilities. With effective self-management strategies, you create a learning environment that makes the most of your learning experience.

Academic-Thinking Strategies

Melanie thinks about course content strategically.

- As she listens to the lecture, she focusses on themes and uses subtitles in her notes to label these major themes.
- Melanie makes time to reread her lecture notes after class, checking that she understands all the main ideas.
- If there are ideas that she does not understand, Melanie tries to clarify the problem by consulting the text, asking another student, or checking with her instructor.

If you are to understand new ideas and learn material in such a way that you can remember and apply it to new situations, you need effective academic-thinking strategies. These are not just a matter of luck. If you are to be a successful student, you will plan ways to think actively about your studies.

Three important goals will guide your planning of thinking strategies:

1. To have good comprehension of the key ideas.
2. To have a good memory of the information.
3. To be able to apply knowledge to new situations.

As you study, it is useful to ask yourself questions that will help you achieve these three goals: "Does this make sense to me? How does this new information relate to concepts that we covered previously in this course? How will I be tested on this information?" Asking questions is an important thinking strategy. As you read this book, you will be asked to think about many academic-thinking strategies. Chapter 5, "Effective Memory," in particular, explores some very important thinking strategies that will enhance long-term retention of essential information.

Strategic Awareness

Strategic awareness refers to Melanie's knowledge about her own ways of learning and also to her ability to co-ordinate appropriate learning strategies. So, not only does Melanie have strategies at her disposal, she also knows a lot about when, where, and how to use them. For example, when Melanie prepared for the history test, she summarized the major concepts into a time line, and she highlighted innovations and other key happenings. Melanie knew that she would need to have this type of important information at her fingertips for the test, so she also devised a mnemonic (memory-aiding) device—in this case an acronym—to help her remember place names that were essential to reporting the sequence of events. Strategies have to be appropriate to the task if they are to be effective, and Melanie devised preparation strategies specific to this test.

As a Good Strategy User, you need to be reflective about your learning strategies. Think about the following questions: Are you able to identify your learning skills strengths? Do you have knowledge of alternative approaches you might take to reviewing for tests? Flexibility of approach is a central characteristic of the Good Strategy User, and the more knowledgeable you are about strategies, the better you can co-ordinate them to meet study demands.

YOU AS A GOOD STRATEGY USER

How do you rate yourself as a Good Strategy User? Choose one course that you are currently taking, and think about the four components of the model.

Name of course: _____

1. Where did your background knowledge come from for this course, and is it adequate for you to keep up with the course material without too much difficulty?

    _____

    _____

    _____

2. How would you describe your general attitude to this course, and what do you believe about your potential to do well in this course?

    _____

    _____

    _____

3. Specify one important self-management strategy and one academic-thinking strategy that you apply to this course.

    Self-management strategy:

    _____

    Academic-thinking strategy:

    _____

4. Give examples of some alternatives available to you in adapting your strategic approach to reading a text chapter if you are very short of time.

_____

_____

_____

WHERE CAN YOU BEGIN?

BEFORE YOU MOVE on to the next chapter, one important point needs to be re-emphasized. Study habits can be very difficult to change, and it is often easier to take the path of least resistance and stay with the comfortable old ways of doing things. When you are trying out a new strategy, it will take a little time before you begin to use it automatically. You may have to generate ways to remind yourself regularly of this new strategy you are trying to adopt. Also, note that not all strategies work for everyone, and you may see friends studying a different way from you. Have confidence that you can evaluate your own learning needs and choose the strategies that are best for you.

This chapter introduced you to the model of the Good Strategy User, which can help you to think about all the factors that have an impact on your learning success. The four components of the Good Strategy User model—background knowledge, personal attitudes and beliefs, learning strategies (self-management and academic-thinking), and strategic awareness—provided you with a systematic framework for evaluating your current approach to learning. Use it if you are having difficulty in a subject. By tracking through the four components of the model, you may be able to pinpoint the source of your problems and identify strategies that can make a difference.

Having introduced you in Part 1 to the idea of strategic learning, the following chapters focus on a wide variety of strategies that cover the major academic tasks that students have to complete. These chapters are organized into three parts: "Self-Management Strategies for Learning," "Strategies for Thinking about Information," and "Effective Application of Knowledge." As you read each chapter, evaluate the strategies that are presented and concentrate on those that you think can make a difference to the quality of your own study techniques.

PART 2

Self-Management Strategies for Learning

CHAPTER 2

Strategies for a Smart Start

LEARNING OBJECTIVES

The purpose of this chapter is for you to:

→ Identify personal resources that can get you off to a smart start.
→ Think about the advantages of working with other students.
→ Consider the importance of getting help from your instructor.
→ Learn how to use your course outlines to your advantage.
→ Think about campus resources that can support your academic success.

T HE WAY YOU start off any school year is important to your academic success and enjoyment as a student. While any new start is a challenge, this is especially true if you are making the major transition from one school to another. There are so many people to meet, things that you have to find out about, decisions to be made, and things to organize. You will need to have some excellent self-management strategies in place early if you are to get off to a smart start.

Chapter 1 introduced the idea of becoming a Good Strategy User. This chapter expands on that idea by suggesting a variety of strategies that you can apply at the beginning of your school year that can get you off to a smart start. The strategies are based on four learning resources: personal learning resources, working with other students, course instructors and outlines, and campus learning resources.

PERSONAL LEARNING RESOURCES

Resources that can help you make a smart start in school begin with you. You alone are the one with the most complete information about your knowledge, skills, interests, attitudes, and the myriad other factors that affect your learning. Therefore, you are your own best resource—better than any of your instructors or counsellors on campus! Before or shortly after your courses begin, you can work on three of your important personal learning resources:

- Academic Program and Course Choices
- Goal-Setting Ability
- Study Environment

Academic Program and Course Choices

Students usually put a lot of thought into their academic program and course choices. They know what background knowledge and skills they need and what time will be required. Most students make good choices, and everything works out well. In other cases, however, students find that their program and/or individual courses are not what they had expected or hoped for, and they don't know what to do about the problem.

As you start your academic year, it is important that you are well informed about your academic program and courses. Hopefully, you will have made the right choices and will not have to make any changes. But if things turn out to be not as you expected, you should be familiar enough with the rules and regulations that you will know what to do.

Study your academic calendar and any other pertinent information about course changes such as the deadlines for adding and dropping courses. The sooner you make necessary changes, the less negative impact there will be. However, if you do make changes, understand clearly all possible implications: Are you closing doors to opportunities that you might regret later? Will your academic status or current level of funding or funding source be affected by the changes you are making?

Goal-Setting Ability

The time to practise your goal-setting ability and to think about the kind of goals that you set is at the beginning of a new term. Without clear goals, there is a good chance that you will just drift along until you suddenly realize that tests are looming and assignments are due, and you have to scramble to meet these deadlines. By setting goals early in the school year, you can avoid this panic.

Long-Term and Short-Term Goals
There are two types of goals: long-term and short-term goals. You will need to set both. For example, without a fairly clear long-term goal such as planning to complete a bachelor's degree, it is difficult to keep up the day-to-day motivation you need to accomplish all your short-term goals such as reading over your notes before putting them in your class binder. However, it is the short-term goals that are most responsible for leading you in the direction of accomplishing your long-term goals. Therefore, in the first few weeks of the term, it is important to practise setting your short-term academic goals.

Content-Oriented and Strategy-Oriented Goals
Short-term goals can be either content or strategy oriented. Content-oriented goals answer the question "What shall I do?" For example, you might say to yourself, "I will finish ten math problems in the next hour." In contrast, strategy-oriented goals answer the question "How can I proceed with this task?" For example, when your content-oriented goal is to solve the math problems, you might say to yourself, as a strategy-oriented goal, "I will first of all review my class notes, redo the solved examples, and then I will attempt the new problems." Many students tend to focus most of their attention on content-oriented academic goals

and give little or no thought to strategy-oriented goals. One of the aims of this book is to help you become a more successful student by emphasizing the importance of short-term strategy-oriented goals.

Getting off to a good start with goal setting will lead to continuing effective goal setting throughout the entire school year. You are more likely to complete your educational goals successfully if you apply the following five principles in the first few weeks of your academic term:

1. Set goals that are specific and measurable: for example, "In the next hour, I will start my essay by creating a working outline and brainstorming a few points for each of the subtopics."
2. Set goals that are positive and realistic: for example, "I will read this anthropology chapter in two-page chunks then summarize the main ideas."
3. Plan ways to remind yourself of the goals you have set. For example, write them somewhere you will see them to remind you of your target.
4. Share your goals with family, friends, and colleagues. They will be more involved in your academic progress if you discuss your goals with them.
5. Establish rewards for the completion of your goals. Planning a treat or some relaxation will reinforce the fact that you have been effective in meeting your goals.

Study Environment

At the beginning of the school year, give some thought to finding a good location for your regular out-of-class study. While your main study location will likely be your residence, try to find other locations around campus that offer the right level of privacy.

If at all possible, a computer should be an integral part of your learning environment. If you do not own one or do not have strong computer skills, investigate the computer facilities available on your campus, and try to set aside some time to learn the basics of word processing, browsing the World Wide Web, using e-mail, or doing calculations on a spreadsheet.

Since there is usually a lot of paper to deal with, you will need to have a reliable filing system for organizing and storing your class notes, handouts, and returned assignments and exams. A Good Strategy User favours a binder for each course, with dividers for filing lecture notes, text summary notes, and other course materials. Separate files for returned assignments, exams, and the like are also a good idea. Set up a system at the beginning of the school year that can be adapted as the year proceeds. Develop the good habit of making back-up copies of any files stored on your computer. You don't want a crashed hard drive to result in the loss of all your work.

WORKING WITH OTHER STUDENTS

Meeting other students is an integral part of your education not just for the social connections, but as a way to enrich your learning. Studying with others can help to motivate you and improve your ability to work as a team player. You can help each other in a variety of ways, such as reminding one another of upcoming tests or changes to the course schedule, discussing the difficulty of a particular assignment, sharing notes, or suggesting other resources.

Find out about opportunities for working with other students either individually or in groups. This strategy may be encouraged by your institution, and there may be study groups in individual courses or in residences. If there are no formal organizations set up for fostering group work, ask around to see if there is interest. Consider these three factors for making the study-group work effective:

1. Choose learning tasks that are appropriate to group work:
   - tasks that are usefully divided into sections such as group projects, team presentations, lab reports, and summaries of supplementary readings or cases;
   - tasks that require a variety of ideas or perspectives such as problem-solving assignments, brainstorming exercises, and exploration of themes; and
   - tasks before exams such as creating and answering possible exam questions, recitation, and explaining a concept to a fellow student.
2. Get clear agreement from each group member on specifics such as scheduling, location, and preparatory tasks. Establish who is responsible for what and when. Groups in which only some members do their work quickly fall apart.
3. Practise group-building behaviour by respecting the input of others and focussing on the task at hand instead of distracting the group with other topics.

COURSE INSTRUCTORS AND OUTLINES

Your course instructors can be valuable learning resources. At first, you may feel a little intimidated by them, especially if you are in large classes, but instructors can provide you with the help you need if you make the effort to see them during their office hours or by appointment. Surprisingly, many course instructors report few visitors during their office hours. By preparing fairly specific questions ahead of time, you can increase the likelihood that the instructor will provide you with useful information. The course outlines provided by your instructors are a road map for the direction of the course and can also be valuable learning resources. When you receive this outline at the beginning of the term, look for the following:

- ☑ your instructor's name, office location, and office hours;
- ☑ the course objectives and your instructor's approach to assignments and exams;
- ☑ a topic outline to indicate the sequence of readings and lectures;
- ☑ the method of evaluation in the course including how the marks are to be allotted;
- ☑ any special instructions about how to complete assignments, essays, labs, etc.; and
- ☑ additional learning resources such as drop-in centres or available tutors.

CAMPUS LEARNING RESOURCES

Most campuses are full of resources that can make a big difference to the quality of the student experience. If you are new to campus, treat yourself to a guided tour, but if that is not available, perhaps you can talk a senior student into showing you around and pointing out useful resources. If even that is not available and you are on your own, pick up a campus map and explore.

Along with the required services offered for admissions and registration, housing, parking, and financial aid, the following campus learning resources can help to ensure a smart start to being a successful student:

- Orientation Sessions
- Learning Skills Services
- Libraries
- Help Centres
- Tutoring Services
- Self-Help Books
- Ombudsperson
- Other Campus Resources

Orientation Sessions

Your campus may offer an orientation program that generally will include an overview of student services, a look at some learning resources, and a campus tour. If there is one, be sure to check it out *before* beginning your courses.

Learning Skills Services

You can usually find at least one counsellor on campus whose main function is to help students learn more efficiently. Usually, learning skills counsellors offer presentations or workshops on learning strategies related to tasks such as lecture note taking, essay writing, text reading, time management, and exam writing. You can also talk to this counsellor about any academic concerns such as poor concentration or test anxiety. Keep in mind that you do not have to be failing a course to take advantage of learning skills services. Whatever your grades, if you are interested in improving your learning strategies, this is the person to talk to.

Libraries

If you are not familiar with your campus libraries, arrange for a guided tour that will acquaint you with the layouts of the buildings, the location of certain collections, the catalogue system, and how to access the services that are provided. Find out how to access your college library through the World Wide Web. The Internet also provides you access to major libraries throughout the world. This is a resource that is revolutionizing access to information.

Help Centres

For some courses or specific skill areas, academic help may be centralized in one location called a learning or help centre (e.g., the Biology Help Centre, Writing Centre, or Math Centre). Ask about what is offered. A learning centre will often have more resources than meets the eye, such as files of old exams, tutorial worksheets, videos, etc. Often learning centres hire quite a few staff who work part time. Meet as many as possible, so that you can find the one or two individuals with whom you can work most effectively. Use the centre regularly to clear up difficulties with your studies as they arise.

Tutoring Services

If you run into serious difficulties with a course, you may wish to use tutoring services. Check with your academic department for names of recommended tutors.

Self-Help Books

This book that you are reading is a good example of a self-help book that encourages you to examine your approach to learning. You can also find books on specific aspects of studying such as essay writing and test taking.

Ombudsperson

The ombudsperson acts as a mediator for students with serious problems with the college or university. For example, if you have an academic problem that cannot be resolved to your satisfaction through the regular channels—a problem with an instructor or concerns about a housing issue—talk to the ombudsperson. You will receive helpful advice and support on your problem as well as suggestions on dealing with it.

Other Campus Resources

There are other campus resources in addition to those that support primarily your academic success. Be a Good Strategy User and find out about what is available and, if necessary, make good use of the following:

- the career resources centre;
- the chaplain's office;
- the international students' office;
- offices for students from minority groups;
- personal counselling;
- student health services; and
- the students' council.

PREPARING FOR YOUR EDUCATIONAL EXPEDITION

A T THE BEGINNING of an academic year, you can anticipate some of the challenges that you need to address as you prepare for your educational journey. Finding the right resources is not always easy because they may be numerous and scattered, especially in colleges and universities. As well, resources may not always be advertised, so you may have to seek them out.

This chapter looked at strategies for a smart start and how you can best prepare for the academic year. It suggested that learning resources are many and that they are found in different places. It began by presenting some basic personal learning resources you will need to succeed. The focus of the chapter then moved outward to strategies for working effectively with other students and for getting the most from your instructors and their course outlines. Finally, this chapter outlined the array of campus learning resources that you can use to help you successfully embark on your educational journey. The next chapter, "Organizing Your Time," continues the theme of self-management strategies by taking a close look at one of the most important issues that falls within the student's personal control: how to manage your time.

CHAPTER 3

Organizing Your Time

LEARNING OBJECTIVES

The purpose of this chapter is for you to:

→ Check your present experience with time management.
→ Learn about the six steps in time management.
→ Apply the steps to your own learning situation.
→ Build flexibility into your time-management system through additional general principles.

DO YOU EVER wonder how the world's great leaders find time to run their countries with only 24 hours in each day? Thinking about such people can help to put things in perspective when you find yourself beginning to panic about not getting things done. Time management is a fact of life for everyone, although there are enormous differences in how individuals make choices about how they will manage time. For some people, time management is little more than responding to things that happen. Others are rigid controllers with definite plans at all times. However, the majority of us are located somewhere in between these two extremes, with many wishing for a more consistent ability to manage time.

This chapter acknowledges that finding the time for everything is a problem you share with most other students. You are invited to assess your current time-management strategies because raising your personal awareness is an important step in taking control of your time planning. This chapter then introduces you to a step-by-step time-management system including principles that will allow you to build flexibility into your basic plan. Flexibility is essential if your time-management plan is to meet your own personal needs in a variety of circumstances. Several problem scenarios illustrate this, with questions following. It is important for you to recognize that the objective of this chapter is not to convert you into a rigid clock watcher, but rather to suggest self-management strategies so that you can achieve better academic results and enjoy your leisure time without feeling guilty. That's what successful time management is all about.

MANAGING TIME EFFECTIVELY IS A COMMON PROBLEM

My friend dropped by last night, and I didn't like to tell him that I had a lot of work to do.

I belong to a couple of clubs, but I find it tough fitting them in with my course load.

It takes me many hours to do all the required reading for my weekly history tutorial.

I work really hard, but I never seem to get everything done that I should.

Practices for the football team are at 4:00 P.M. each day, and I don't get home until 7:00 P.M. By the time I finish my supper, I am ready for a nap.

Students commonly report dissatisfaction with their personal attempts at time management. Those above are describing a number of different problems. First, there are unexpected events that have not been planned for, such as the visit of a friend. Then there is the challenge of finding time for more than just studying. Time for extra-curricular activities such as membership in clubs or participation in sports teams requires planning so that study time can be balanced with other interests. Many students identify with the experience of tasks taking longer than planned, leading to the feeling that they are getting nowhere. However hard they work, they feel as though there are a million other things still to be done.

HOW DO YOU CURRENTLY MANAGE YOUR TIME?

For each question, check the response that best fits your personal experience. After you have finished the exercise, you may wish to reflect on your overall satisfaction with your current time-management efforts.

For each item, check one of the following:
1 = NO; 2 = SOMETIMES; 3 = YES

	1	2	3
1. Do you have a system for planning each day?	___	___	___
2. Do you feel pressured by others to join in their activities?	___	___	___
3. Do you have time to do the things you want to do?	___	___	___
4. Do you really worry about getting things done?	___	___	___
5. Do you feel in control of your schedule?	___	___	___
6. Is time management a problem for you?	___	___	___
7. Do your own friends practise good time management?	___	___	___
8. Do you find yourself racing from one deadline to another?	___	___	___
9. Do you have a clear idea of where your time goes?	___	___	___

10. Are you too busy to eat properly or exercise regularly?
11. Do you talk with friends and instructors about time-management problems?
12. Do things often pile up?
13. Do you feel that your marks reflect good time management?

1	2	3
___	___	___
___	___	___
___	___	___
___	___	___

If you answered NO to any odd-numbered items or YES to any even-numbered items, chances are that there are strategies in your time-management system that could be improved.

A STEP-BY-STEP TIME-MANAGEMENT SYSTEM

By following the step-by-step time-management system, you can take control of time and make it work to your advantage. We will now discuss the following six recommended steps:

- Step 1: Decide to Improve Your Time Management
- Step 2: Make a Careful Assessment of Your Current Activities
- Step 3: Plan Ahead and Keep a Schedule
- Step 4: Choose an Appropriate Study Environment
- Step 5: Make the Most of Each Study Session
- Step 6: Evaluate Your Time-Management Plan Regularly

Step 1: Decide to Improve Your Time Management

Before you can implement an effective personal time-management system, you have to decide that you want to take control over your time. Begin by being very honest with yourself in your assessment of how successful you are at managing your time. What system do you use? Does it work for you? If your answer is "Yes, my system does work for me," then what do you see as the strengths of your system? If your answer is "No, I am not a good time planner," what are the problems as you see them?

1. What are some of the main components of your current time-management plan?

   _____

   _____

2. What works well with your current system?

   _____

   _____

3. What problems are there with your current system?

   _____

   _____

4. How motivated are you to learn about and apply time-management strategies? Rank yourself on a scale of 1 (not motivated) to 10 (highly motivated).

   1   2   3   4   5   6   7   8   9   10

Many students want to be good time managers but lack the self-management necessary to follow through adequately on their plans. Although others can give you encouragement, you are the one in charge, and you have to make the decision to manage your time and to follow through on your plans. If you feel motivated at this point to give a systematic time-management plan a try, continue with the following steps to effective personal time management.

Step 2: Make a Careful Assessment of Your Current Activities

Use Table 3.1 to gather information on your activities. In your mind, go over a couple of typical days and try not to miss any essential activities. For example, students sometimes forget to include travel time, which can represent a significant amount of time! Then complete the table, using the following checklist as a guide.

☑ List all the activities that you must, or would like to, find time for.
☑ Estimate how much time (hours per week) each activity will require.
☑ Will each activity take place regularly or occasionally?
☑ Label each activity as either essential or optional.
☑ Rank each activity on a scale of high/medium/low priority.

When you have completed the table, look over the activities and give yourself time to digest the information that you have gathered. A major difficulty for many students is making choices. You may find that you have listed more activities than you have time for. What choices do you have? Can you limit your activities to a manageable combination?

TABLE 3.1 ASSESSMENT OF CURRENT ACTIVITIES

Activities	Hours per Week	Regular or Occasional	Essential or Optional	Priority: High/ Medium/ Low

Your most important choices have to do with your academic program (for example, the course load you wish to take). In some programs, you have no choice, and you have to take a full load of courses. If you want to play on a school sports team, there may be mandatory academic requirements that you have to meet. If you are paying for your education by working at a part-time job, you should seriously consider reducing your course load if you work more than ten hours per week. These are just a few situations that require careful planning.

In this step of your time-management plan, you need to find the right balance of academic work and other activities. If you overload your academic activities, you may find that you tend to lose energy because you are not taking time to recharge your batteries. On the other hand, if you overdo your nonacademic work, sports, or social activities, you will soon fall behind with the necessary school work and will find tests and assignments to be intimidating experiences. Good choices are essential to reaching your academic potential, and you are in charge of those choices.

Step 3: Plan Ahead and Keep a Schedule

Few people can be really successful students if they do not plan ahead for key events. When you record the dates of tests, assignments, and other personal commitments, you are more likely to follow through and do the necessary work. More importantly, perhaps, is to select and enter in a calendar or day planner the dates when you are going to begin work on that big assignment or start studying for that crucial test. Place a wall calendar in a prominent location, and get in the habit of always carrying your day planner or organizer with your academic books and binders.

Even if you have never before been a systematic time planner, this is the time to try out the system and to invest in a wall calendar (or two) and a personal day planner or organizer. There are many different styles for you to choose from, and some schools provide day planners free to their students. You might design a weekly timetable and a term-long calendar on your computer or hand-held organizer. There are many software programs that can help.

As soon as you get your course outlines, review them for significant dates and deadlines and enter these in your planner. Also, listen in class for additional information that may not have been available in the course outline, and add any new dates to your planner.

☑ Plan for the term and mark important assignment and test dates on a wall calendar. Also add your start dates for working on those assignments or studying for those tests. Pay special attention to any weeks that appear to be overloaded; you may need to get an early start for some of the activities.

☑ Also, add any dates for important nonacademic activities, and try to maintain a balance with your academic activities. You need to monitor the amount of time you are spending on activities such as committees, fitness and recreation activities, or at a part-time job. If you plan far enough in advance, you can often make adjustments so that they do not interfere with high-priority academic commitments.

☑ Post a weekly timetable in a prominent location with all of your regular class times indicated. Indicate (maybe in red) some blocks of time that you are going to reserve on a regular basis for out-of-class study. If you can develop a regular study timetable, you will find that your work gets completed and that you feel in control of all of your work.

☑ Use a day planner or other system to plan a tentative schedule of study tasks that you wish to accomplish in a week. You may not always follow the schedule rigidly, but it will guide your daily planning. Keep in mind two key strategies: (a) your best times of day to study, and (b) using small blocks of time between other activities. Look at the sample of a weekly timetable that was created by a student (Table 3.2). Then use the blank weekly timetable (Table 3.3) to plan a week of studying.

☑ Each evening, think about what you want to get done the next day, and record your study tasks for that day. Collect together all necessary notes and texts that you will need to follow through on your plans.

TABLE 3.2 COMPLETED WEEKLY TIMETABLE

	Monday	Tuesday	Wednesday	Thursday	Friday	Saturday	Sunday
7:00-8:00	←		Breakfast		→		
8:00-9:00		↑		Math Tutorial	↑ Geog Lab		
9:00-10:00		Bio Lab	↑		↓		
10:00-11:00		↓	Chem Lab				
11:00-12:00	Swim	Geog 020	↓	Geog 020	Lunch		
12:00-1:00	Math 027	Lunch	Math 027	Lunch	Math 027		
1:00-2:00	Lunch	Physics 020	Lunch	Physics 020			
2:00-3:00	Chem 020		Chem 020	↑			
3:00-4:00	↑ Bio 020		Squash	Physics Lab			
4:00-5:00	↓	Swim	Swim	↓	Swim		
5:00-6:00	←		Dinner		→		
6:00-7:00				↑			
7:00-8:00				Squash Club			
8:00-9:00				↓			
9:00-10:00							
10:00-11:00							

☐ Planned Study Time   ⸬ Flexible Study Time

TABLE 3.3 BLANK WEEKLY TIMETABLE

	Monday	Tuesday	Wednesday	Thursday	Friday	Saturday	Sunday
7:00-8:00							
8:00-9:00							
9:00-10:00							
10:00-11:00							
11:00-12:00							
12:00-1:00							
1:00-2:00							
2:00-3:00							
3:00-4:00							
4:00-5:00							
5:00-6:00							
6:00-7:00							
7:00-8:00							
8:00-9:00							
9:00-10:00							
10:00-11:00							

Step 4: Choose an Appropriate Study Environment

A crucial element to accomplishing your study goals is the out-of-class learning environment that you establish in which you can concentrate and get things done. This applies regardless of whether you live at home, in a rented apartment, or in a student residence. We often hear students complaining about how difficult it is to work because people around them are distracting. However, one student wisely said that "if someone really wants to work, he can always find the right place, even if it means going into one of those often underused libraries!"

☑ Find a quiet, comfortable place to study.
☑ Make sure that you have all the necessary materials and equipment.
☑ Check your study tasks for the day.
☑ Set a study goal for what you wish to accomplish in the next short time period (twenty to fifty minutes).

Step 5: Make the Most of Each Study Session

When you sit down to study, give your full attention to getting the most out of the time you have. You will want to maximize your level of concentration so that you can move along with the study task as efficiently as possible. You will get a great sense of achievement if you can optimize each work session. There is nothing worse than spending several hours at a desk and knowing that you have wasted a good chunk of that time in daydreaming or worrying. If this is a common problem for you, then read the next chapter, "Managing the Stress of Being a Student," very carefully.

☑ Get started on your work quickly.
☑ Work to achieve each study goal you have set.
☑ Take small appropriate breaks to keep your energy and concentration levels high.
☑ Check off the tasks in your daily planner as you complete them.

Step 6: Evaluate Your Time-Management Plan Regularly

One common characteristic of plans is that they may need to be adjusted—often in relatively small ways, but sometimes in rather major ways. If you are not meeting your study goals, what are the reasons? If it is because you failed to follow through with your study plans, you may need to remind yourself of your academic goals and your motivation to do well. Think about how you can be more successful at meeting your goals in the coming week, and reset some manageable goals.

If you were putting in a real effort but just couldn't meet your goals, try the following:

- ☑ Prioritize the most important tasks and reschedule those that need more time to complete.
- ☑ Adjust your tentative schedule for the remainder of the week.
- ☑ Think creatively about how you are completing tasks. Can you think of any timesavers?
- ☑ If you continually experience real time-management problems, monitor your activities carefully, and decide if you can make constructive adjustments by yourself. If you are not happy with how things are going, seek help from your instructor or learning skills counsellor.

RECORDING AND ANALYZING TIME SPENT

If you are having difficulties with time management, monitor your time for three typical weekdays. Use Table 3.4 to record your activities hour by hour. Pay particular attention to out-of-class study time. Use this information to find out how much time you are spending on different activities by completing Table 3.5. You may be able to adjust your planning based on this information. It will also be a useful starting point for getting help from your instructor or counsellor.

TABLE 3.4 BLANK TIMETABLE FOR ANALYZING TIME SPENT

	Monday	Tuesday	Wednesday	Thursday	Friday
7:00					
8:00					
9:00					
10:00					
11:00					
12:00					
1:00					
2:00					
3:00					
4:00					
5:00					
6:00					
7:00					
8:00					
9:00					
10:00					
11:00					

TABLE 3.5   ANALYSIS OF THREE STUDY DAYS

ACTIVITIES	HOURS			
	Day 1	Day 2	Day 3	Total
Class				
Study				
Travel				
Exercise				
Meals and Chores				
Leisure				
Sleep				
TOTAL				

1. Fill in the total hours of study time for each course. List the tasks that were done.

COURSE	HOURS	TASKS
1.		
2.		
3.		
4.		
5.		

2. Can you see which times of the day are good for

   • serious concentration? _____

   • less-demanding study tasks? _____

3. Can you detect a time that is not productive for studying?

   _____

BUILDING FLEXIBILITY INTO YOUR TIME-MANAGEMENT SYSTEM

In addition to having a time-management system (based on the fundamental principles of setting priorities, maintaining a balance of academic and nonacademic activities, planning ahead, and keeping a schedule), applying the following additional time-management principles can help you to maintain the momentum of your system as well as adapt it to meet additional needs if necessary:

- Make Each Day Count
- Know and Use Your Best Times
- Use Small Blocks of Time
- Plan for Meals and Recreation
- Plan Adequate Study Time for Courses You Dislike
- Review Your Lecture Notes Soon after the Class
- Spread Out Learning of Memory Material
- Organize Extended Learning for Project Tasks

Make Each Day Count

Aim to get some high-priority tasks completed each day. Even small, regular accomplishments can make a big hole in the total amount that you have to get done. Some time managers refer to this as the "Swiss cheese" approach.

Know and Use Your Best Times

It is likely that there are certain times in each day when you are more able to do tasks efficiently that require concentration. In contrast, there may be other times of the day when it is more difficult for you to make progress. When are your best times for studying? Whenever possible, do you try to use these times for studying rather than for less important activities?

Try to avoid the habit of studying only late at night because this is when other people are not around to interrupt you. Although many students believe that nighttime is when they are most mentally alert, medical evidence does not support this opinion. Most people are more alert during daytime hours.

Use Small Blocks of Time

Many useful hours in the week are wasted by students who think that an hour between classes is not enough time to get anything accomplished. You can do a good deal of important work in an hour or less: reviewing class notes, reading part of a chapter, doing a few math problems, going to see an instructor. A number of successful students report that this is their most important time-management strategy.

Plan for Meals and Recreation

Although it is important to look after your academic needs, it is equally important to look after other needs. A healthy lifestyle is crucial to enjoyment of student life and to your ability to study effectively. However, this also requires some planning. Make time for nutritious meals (especially a breakfast with some protein), regular exercise, and a reasonable amount of time for relaxation. Unfortunately, many students, in a futile effort to get more done, get into the vicious circle of short-changing their health and thus their effectiveness. This is particularly prevalent during exams. However, it is even more crucial that you get exercise, eat well, and get enough sleep during exams because it is during this time that students are under more stress and require extra energy.

Plan Adequate Study Time for Courses You Dislike

This strategy is mentioned specifically because so many students make the mistake of studying long hours on courses they like and putting little time into courses they dislike. Because these students have "studied a lot" in general, they are often surprised when they do poorly on the courses they dislike.

Review Your Lecture Notes Soon after the Class

Brief, same-day review of lecture notes can be a very powerful timesaving strategy. This is particularly true if your notes are not as complete or organized as they might be. Retyping your notes onto your computer might help you to clarify the ideas. However, this should only be necessary for class notes that are not in good shape. By doing some kind of active but brief review of your lecture notes on or near the day of that lecture, you can save many hours of "relearning." (See Chapter 6, "Learning from Lectures," for more details.)

Spread Out Learning of Memory Material

With courses in which you need to memorize detailed information such as biology, psychology, or economics, you will be more successful if you spread your learning over a number of separate study periods. Three one-hour study periods throughout the week will be more effective for you than a single three-hour chunk.

Organize Extended Learning for Project Tasks

You should tackle project tasks such as essays, case studies, and lab reports over a fairly extended period of time because these activities often require you to integrate a variety of sources in order to accomplish deeper levels of insight and organization. Even within such extended learning periods, it is still useful to set up subgoals and take short breaks.

TIME-MANAGEMENT PROBLEM SCENARIOS

Andrew has been spending more and more of his time talking with his friends than preparing for his classes. He's frequently so involved that he forgets to go to his lectures. He often says he has problems controlling his time. What suggestions do you have for Andrew?

_____

_____

Maria, a first-year student, is taking six courses. She feels a great amount of pressure because her family has sacrificed for her education. She's having difficulty managing her time, and now she has been offered a part-time job. What comments would you make on Maria's situation?

_____

_____

Michele has come to university to meet new people and expand her horizons. Her studies are important to her, but she also wants to have an active social life. This is the second week of class and Michele hasn't done any studying so far. If you were to meet Michele, what advice and help would you offer her?

_____

_____

Daniel would like to be on the student council. He also wants to get into medical school and is in a demanding first-year science program. How can Daniel accommodate these two goals?

_____

_____

SUCCESSFUL TIME MANAGEMENT

THE TWO MAJOR challenges that you face in managing your time will be: first, to find the right balance between your academic and nonacademic activities; and second, to apply yourself consistently to those activities that will lead to success. If you can meet these challenges, your years in school will be very rewarding as you grow both academically and socially as part of a broader community. Further, the time-management skills that you develop and that work for you as a student will stay with you and enhance your later work and personal life.

This chapter stressed self-management of time and led you through a six-step process that included exploring your motivation, assessing your current activities, and planning, implementing, and evaluating your time-management system. Maintaining the system and adding flexibility can be built in by regularly applying general principles of time management. You stand to gain greatly by having sound time management in place. For those for whom time management is a constant challenge, the following chapter, "Managing the Stress of Being a Student," addresses the twin issues of good concentration and beating procrastination.

CHAPTER 4

Managing the Stress of Being a Student

LEARNING OBJECTIVES

The purpose of this chapter is for you to:

→ Learn how to identify your symptoms of stress.
→ Identify strategies that can help you to cope with stress.
→ Recognize the importance of good concentration.
→ Select strategies that will help you achieve good concentration.
→ Learn about examples of and reasons for procrastination.
→ Select strategies that you can use to overcome procrastination.

MANY STUDENTS REPORT that they experience symptoms of stress as they try to balance the demands of being a student with their physical and mental capacity to sustain wear and tear. You may identify with this problem. Each new school year can bring with it potential sources of stress for you, especially if you move to a different school and have to find your way around campus and meet new students and instructors.

This chapter discusses ways in which you can recognize your own responses to stress. It prompts you to realize that your stress responses frequently reflect your mental messages about the demands of specific events and situations. This chapter also presents a variety of strategies that you can practise in order to reduce the psychological and physical symptoms of stress that you may experience as a student. If you can identify effective ways of relieving tension, you will feel more motivated to study and more in control of your school experience.

WHAT IS STRESS?

Anyone who feels stress usually feels emotional discomfort and concern about not being able to cope. At a physical level, this may mean loss of appetite, sleeplessness, headaches, sweating, and ulcers or other illnesses. At a psychological level, this may involve feeling helpless, anxious, or afraid of losing control. Such feelings can trigger a number of subtle chemical changes in the brain and the immune system and can lower your body's ability to cope with day-to-day strain and to fight off infection.

Although everyone experiences stress from time to time, the level of stress that individuals experience from the same situation varies greatly. For example, a snowstorm is not stressful to a skier, but it is to someone who has to drive any distance to an important meeting. The skier will probably experience what Hans Selye[2] has described as "eu-stress"—a positive response as she thinks about a day on the ski slopes. The driver, however, will experience distress—a negative response to the snowstorm as she imagines being unable to reach the meeting on time.

---

[2] Selye, H. (1978). *The stress of life* (2nd ed.). New York: McGraw-Hill.

The way that you interpret events is of critical importance to the way you respond to them. When you are devising strategies to deal with stress, it is important to recognize the importance of your perceptions about the events going on around you.

STRATEGIES FOR COPING WITH STRESS

A number of personal factors have been attributed to a person's ability to handle stressful events effectively, including:

- having a sense of control over his or her life;
- having a network of friends and family to provide support;
- having a flexible attitude to unexpected events; and
- regularly engaging in a hobby, sport, or outside interest.

However, many people, at some time or other in their lives, find that stress is a debilitating factor. They need to put into place appropriate coping strategies if stress is to be maintained at reasonable levels. If there is no obvious trigger for the stress they are experiencing, they might begin by monitoring and even recording their physical symptoms to try to identify which situations prompt the stress response. If they can see a pattern and recognize the most stressful events, they can then start to explain what threats or pressures trigger anxiety and learn to deal with them.

There may be times when problems feel overwhelming, and however hard you try, you can't shake off severe anxiety and depression. Schools, colleges, and universities have professional staff who can help you. Sharing your worries and discussing solutions with another person, either a counsellor or a health professional, can make a positive difference. Don't hesitate to seek help from others if you need it.

Psychological Strategies for Coping with Stress

The way you think about events can have a powerful influence on whether you find them stressful. Since your thoughts influence your response to stress, try to recognize your inner dialogue about day-to-day demands and expectations. Many of us are not aware of our "self-talk" and do not realize how self-defeating it may be. For example, if you dread certain occasions and fear their possible consequences (e.g., presenting a seminar), it will be difficult to control your negative reactions and to work on preparing an effective seminar presentation.

Worried thoughts are not only distracting, but can also lead to physical symptoms of stress such as tension headaches, sleeplessness, and upset stomach. You might begin by comparing your mental messages about studying with thoughts about something that you really enjoy. Record what your thoughts might be in the situations listed in Table 4.1.

When you are enjoying an activity, you are usually less concerned about making mistakes, your own limitations, or future consequences. In contrast, when you are anxious about your academic progress, your worries can distract your attention and interfere with learning. This may prompt you to take time out to rest, but that may be a temporary solution. You still have to find a way to put positive energy into studying. One self-management strategy that can help is to focus your thoughts on the present with statements such as "What's involved here?" or "What's the next step?"

TABLE 4.1 YOUR RECORDED THOUGHTS

Your Experience	Study Activity (e.g., thoughts while writing an in-class test)	Leisure Activity (e.g., thoughts while playing tennis with a friend)
You make a mistake		
You recognize your limitations to do well		
You consider the future consequences of this event		

Physical Strategies for Coping with Stress

In addition to considering the psychological aspects of stress, it is also important to evaluate how to keep in good physical shape to handle pressure.

Find Ways to Become a More Relaxed Person
- ☑ Learn relaxation techniques to reduce tension. You can practise deep breathing or yoga, take a warm bath, or listen to some of your favourite music.
- ☑ Take regular and planned breaks from studying.
- ☑ If you begin to panic, remove yourself from the source of stress. Get up from your desk and take a short walk.
- ☑ Take up a sport, hobby, or part-time interest that will help you to relax.

Develop a Healthy Lifestyle Ensuring That You Eat and Sleep Regularly
- ☑ Plan to eat with friends to maintain your social contacts.
- ☑ Take a positive attitude toward your body image. Being preoccupied with your weight or appearance can be a source of a lot of stress.
- ☑ Try to eat a variety of foods necessary for a regularly balanced diet.
- ☑ Maintain a sensible sleep routine. Don't try to escape stress by oversleeping during the day.

CONCENTRATION

Poor concentration can be the source of real stress for many students. They may be very motivated to work and yet find their minds dreaming about anything but school. Good concentration is very important to make study time most effective. Two or three hours of intense effort are worth a day of interrupted or haphazard study. Concentration does not "just happen." Good Strategy Users are aware of those components of concentration that are within their control. A strategic approach can result in increased concentration and better academic performance. How can some students sit down and concentrate fully whereas others find themselves daydreaming or being distracted by disturbances around them? There are three components of concentration for you to consider:

- Commitment
- Internal Distractions
- External Distractions

Commitment

Your level of commitment while studying is closely linked to your interest in the subject matter, the way in which the course is taught, the setting, and whether or not it is an optional or mandatory course. The following strategies can help you to maintain a high level of commitment to a course:

- **Find out as much as you can about a course before choosing to take it.** Read the calendar description, talk to the instructor, and, if possible, talk to students who have taken the course. Check that your background is adequate to enable you to handle the course without any major problems and that you feel confident about the workload.
- **Assess the contribution that the course will make** to your general knowledge, to your degree program, and to possible career choices. Your commitment will be stronger if you have a clear idea about the benefits of the course.
- **Know the rules and regulations governing the course.** If you have a clear idea of whether or not you can withdraw from a course if things go poorly, you will not feel so trapped and be better able to give it a reasonable effort.
- **If you anticipate any problems, you may wish to be part of a study group.** In difficult courses, it can be helpful for students to meet to share ideas and study tasks.
- **Try to work regularly at the course.** It is difficult to maintain a high level of commitment when you fall behind and get overwhelmed by the amount of work.
- **Try to generate interest in a required course.** You might try to find out about the history of the course or talk about it with someone who seems to enjoy it.

Internal Distractions

You will lose concentration while studying if you are uncomfortable physically. You may be too hot, too hungry, or too full. The light level may be straining your eyes, or the position in which you are studying may cause your neck or back to hurt. Consequently, you may find that you begin to think about a whole range of different things, none of them associated with the course material. Setting the environment for study is important to managing concentration. Your determination to pursue your studying in an active way can be gauged by whether or not you can use some of the following self-management strategies to control internal distractions and increase your level of concentration:

- **Define a specific objective to be completed in a limited time frame.** This can avoid the vagueness of an approach such as "I'll do as much as I can on Tuesday evening." In contrast, saying "I'm going to read five pages of sociology and make up three questions" can give you realistic goals to work toward.
- **Set up a method of self-testing the work you have covered in any hour.** Knowing that you have to self-test will keep your focus on the task. The self-testing activities will increase your ability to recall material.
- **When your mind wanders from the topic at hand, put a check mark on a piece of paper.** Monitoring the number of check marks you accumulate over several study sessions will allow you to monitor whether or not your attention span is improving.
- **Try "thought stopping" when you find yourself daydreaming.** Some reflection, especially if some personal emergencies are interfering with study, can be productive. However, if this happens too often, say "STOP" mentally and then redirect your attention back to the work you are doing.
- **Use problem-solving techniques to deal with a persistently disturbing thought** such as "Should I be looking for a part-time job?" Try this approach:
  - ☑ Move away from your study task.
  - ☑ Decide what is bothering you.
  - ☑ Look at why the issue is nagging away at you.
  - ☑ List the pros and cons of possible solutions to the problem.
  - ☑ Decide whether you can handle the issue by yourself or whether you need to consult with others.
  - ☑ Plan when and how to deal with this particular problem. Make a note of it, and then return to your studying.

External Distractions

Although finding a time and place for studying with few distractions will not guarantee concentration, it can make it easier for you to control your attention. Most of us can focus on only one main train of thought at a time. In your study experience, how difficult do you find it to ignore the distractions listed in Table 4.2?

Students will give different answers to this list although few can ignore being interrupted by someone. Students who regularly work well in a particular setting learn to expect to concentrate in that place. This also holds true for getting used to working at certain times of the day. Maintaining concentration will be easier if you:

TABLE 4.2 MONITOR YOUR DISTRACTIONS

		Easy to Ignore	More Difficult to Ignore	Impossible to Ignore
1.	Hearing a conversation near your desk.			
2.	Sensing doors opening and shutting.			
3.	Hearing the radio or TV in the room.			
4.	Noticing traffic outside the room.			
5.	Hearing specific loud noises (e.g., a siren).			
6.	Being interrupted by someone.			

- **Clear your desk of souvenirs, pictures, etc.** These can be extremely distracting.
- **Arrange your desk so that it faces a blank wall.** Even your studying should be more interesting than a blank wall!
- **Know which libraries suit you.** Experiment until you find the ones in which you prefer to study.
- **Have the right level of noise in the background.** Some students claim that they work better with a level of "white noise"; others like silence. Try different situations.

YOUR CONCENTRATION PROFILE

Assume that you want to give your full concentration to a task. In the space below, describe the ideal situation that will allow you complete concentration.

_____

_____

_____

At one time or another, we all have problems concentrating on a task. Imagine you are reading a chapter in a chemistry or sociology text. Even though the environment is conducive to studying, after twenty minutes you feel like giving up because you realize that you are not getting anything out of it. List some possible reasons for this.

_____

_____

_____

PROCRASTINATION

Procrastination can be both the cause and the result of academic stress for many students. Understanding procrastination is not easy because it is a complex behaviour. Just about every student procrastinates on occasion. The reasons for this behaviour as well as the forms it takes are almost as varied as the students themselves.

Symptoms of Procrastination

- **Feelings of inertia.** You do not feel like doing anything, especially school work, even if it is critical that it be done. It takes less energy to continue with the same activity—especially if it is having a cup of coffee or watching TV—than to find the energy to begin something new.
- **Preoccupation with minor tasks or "loose ends."** You feel it is important to finish one thing completely before going on to another. Sometimes there are so many small tasks to complete that the larger and more important tasks are ignored until it is too late to do a good job.
- **Being swamped with work.** With many things to do, all claiming equal priority, it is hard to decide where to begin. As you evaluate all the study tasks to be done, you may get overwhelmed and take the line of least resistance: not to get started on anything.
- **Overinvolvement in other activities.** Other activities (e.g., sports, socializing, movies) seem to have more payoff than studying, especially in the short term.

- **Seeking the company of others.** Like many tasks, studying is isolating. It has to be done alone. If you are feeling lonely and looking for an excuse not to work, you may go looking for someone to talk to instead of getting down to work.
- **Feelings of guilt.** What is being neglected for study? Other things require your time and attention—your friends, family, church, the dog. To some people, taking time to study may seem to be taking time away from others. Guilt feelings interfere with thought processes, and you get nothing done.
- **Confusion.** It is not uncommon for students to report that they are feeling confused about certain assignments that they have to complete. For example, with an essay assignment, you may be confused about the nature and scope of the topic under investigation or how to identify the thesis statement or incorporate reference material. It's easier to put it aside than try to figure it out.

UNDERSTANDING PROCRASTINATION

Students can be adept at finding activities other than studying that appear to be worthwhile: spending time at the gym (it's good to be fit), participating in club activities (great experience on the résumé), and volunteering (valuable career exploration). However, these useful activities can all be substitutes for studying. Most students can think of more conscientious ways to get more work done, but they have difficulty translating these into action. If you feel that you procrastinate regularly, then you need to ask yourself some questions. "What function does procrastination play?" "Why do I want to avoid studying?" Three explanations for procrastination that you might consider are:

- Fear of Failure
- Fear of Success
- Avoidance of Control

Fear of Failure

Many students have doubts about whether they can be successful in a course. By procrastinating, they give themselves an excuse for not performing well by putting in too little time to do the necessary work. If a student does work hard but does not get a good grade, then it is possible that the student does not have the necessary skill or ability—a much more difficult realization than attributing a poor grade to lack of effort. Students who are afraid of failure may be perfectionists with very high standards who are understandably afraid that whatever they do will not be good enough.

Fear of Success

Some students put off making a serious commitment to study for a course because they anticipate, either consciously or unconsciously, unpleasant consequences from doing well. For example, they may fear that their relationship with classmates will suffer. Parents, a partner, or the instructor may expect even higher standards of performance in the future and exert increased pressure. Personal expectations and accompanying stress levels may rise. Consequently, students may decide that life will be simpler if studying gets less effort. The negative side of this is that students will not reach their potential performance level.

Avoidance of Control

Some students feel too controlled by others—instructors, parents, or the school rules. They realize that they are expected to meet the educational challenge, which may seem much too predictable to a student who wants to establish an independent identity. In the short term, not making an effort to study appears to be a way of taking control and "rebelling." It seems to be especially appealing to those who may have been pressured to achieve in elementary or high school or who are unsure about their choice of program.

REMEDIES FOR PROCRASTINATION

There are several ways to combat procrastination. Below are some suggestions.

☑ Substitute the mental message "I should" with "I'd like to."
☑ Set up a reward for finishing something. This can counteract lack of initiative.

(continued)

(continued)

☑ Begin to work on a study task that is not too demanding.
☑ Subdivide a bigger task into several smaller chunks, say, fifteen-minute items. This can reduce the level of difficulty of the overall task.
☑ Suspend your criticism about how well you are doing in order to complete a task for the first time.
☑ Co-operate with a friend to share a task and to reduce isolation.

YOU AND PROCRASTINATION

What are the symptoms of procrastination that you display?

_____

_____

_____

Can you give any reasons for the times when you did procrastinate?

_____

_____

_____

What can you do to make sure that procrastination does not have a negative effect on your academic performance?

_____

_____

_____

_____

CAN YOU HELP SOLVE THE PROBLEMS?

Raj is feeling that his world is falling apart. He worked so hard for a test but got a mediocre mark. Now he feels that his dream of getting into law school is fading and that life is hopeless. What can he do?

_____

_____

_____

Doris had started back to school with such high hopes. It had been twenty years since she had been in school. This first essay was such a struggle, and her grade reflects that. She barely passed and is feeling very stressed out. How can she get her confidence back?

_____

_____

_____

David just cannot get started on his geography lab assignment. He knows exactly what he has to do, but finding the enthusiasm for all that map work is not easy. He does not like the instructor or the course. How can he handle this dilemma?

_____

_____

_____

Megan is daydreaming in the library again. Every time she hears someone go by, she looks up. Then she tries to focus again on reading about the Canadian Constitution. She can hardly wait for 5:00 so she can pack up and go home. Any suggestions for Megan?

_____

_____

_____

CONTROLLING YOUR LEVEL OF STRESS

THIS CHAPTER DISCUSSED how you can become more aware of your responses to stress. It presented self-management strategies, both psychological and physical, to help you cope with symptoms of stress. If you can commit yourself to your studies and avoid internal and external distractions, you will be more likely to achieve good concentration and effective thinking strategies.

This chapter also talked about how students procrastinate, which can, in itself, become a major source of stress. It suggested strategies to help you divide your study time into manageable tasks. Finally, it recommended that students who feel anxious about the demands of their academic courses should ask for help in assessing how to develop strategies to achieve better concentration and control over their response to pressure.

This part of *Learning for Success* has explored self-management strategies. It has emphasized the importance of mobilizing a variety of resources at the beginning of any new term, introduced a systematic plan for time management, and has taken a close look at managing the stress that is so often a part of student life. There is a change of focus in the third part of this book. It will present the key information-processing strategies that are necessary for effective learning. The next chapter introduces this new part as it looks at effective memory.

PART 3

Strategies for Thinking about Information

CHAPTER 5

Effective Memory

LEARNING OBJECTIVES

The purpose of this chapter is for you to:

→ Learn about three memory systems and their relevance to you as a learner.
→ Structure information into a meaningful pattern through an exercise.
→ Apply the ideas of structuring information and identifying patterns.
→ Learn how to improve memory storage.

S TUDENTS COMMONLY REPORT problems with memory. Many describe how they can understand new ideas, but later the information just doesn't stick. Students also commonly report that their friends can remember everything without any effort at all, and how they feel frustration with their own memory when a friend gets a higher grade without, seemingly, having studied much at all. While there are undoubtedly differences among students in the ease with which information is retained, there are strategies that can be applied that can improve retention over the long term. To be able to apply effective memory strategies, one needs first to understand some current theory about memory that can help to explain memory problems.

This chapter begins by examining how three types of memory are thought to operate together and what this implies for the learner. It then goes on to explore ways in which memory is stored to improve retrieval. The main purpose of this chapter is to have you relate the theory about memory systems to your own learning experience. As you read, ask yourself the following questions: "How does this theory reflect my own way of studying? In the light of these theories, what changes do I need to make to the way in which I study? What do I need to do to build these ideas into my own learning strategies?"

MEMORY SYSTEMS

Educators distinguish three memory systems operating together but each with distinct characteristics and functions (see Figure 5.1). They are described very briefly here, focussing on the major implications for any learner wishing to take more personal control over the learning process. The three memory systems are:

- Sensory Memory
- Short-Term Memory
- Long-Term Memory

Sensory Memory

Our senses—sight, hearing, touch, taste, smell, and sense of position—register information from our environment. An important feature of the sensory-memory

FIGURE 5.1 A THEORETICAL VIEW OF MEMORY

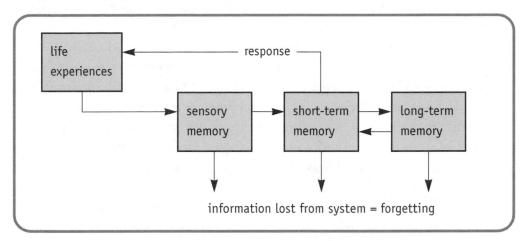

system is that the senses register information only for an instant. It is then either forgotten or is passed on to short-term memory as a conscious thought. How is this significant to you as a learner? Well, you might view sensory memory as a critical gateway through which information must pass in order to be available to your short-term memory. For information to register in short-term memory, you must attend to and concentrate on it.

In everyday life, if you could register all of the stimuli available to your sensory-memory system, your senses would become overloaded. When you sit at a desk processing some lecture notes, for example, you do not usually notice the pressure of your feet on the floor or hear background noises around you such as a fan or traffic outside. To be a Good Strategy User, you need to develop the ability to limit your attention to critical and necessary stimuli. Much of what your sensory memory does register is related to goals that you set. In other words, your immediate learning goals have a profound effect on the information that passes from your sensory to your short-term memory.

Short-Term Memory

Short-term memory is sometimes referred to as working memory because it is here that you actively work to make sense of and respond to stimuli entering from the sensory memory environment or from knowledge you retrieve from long-term storage.

Two characteristics of short-term memory are critical to you as a learner. The first is that you lose information very quickly by forgetting unless you process the information further in some way (e.g., by reciting a telephone number over and over again in your head if something stops you from dialling the number immediately). The second is that it has limited capacity. When new information enters the memory, it often displaces what is already there in short-term memory. For example, switching between the simultaneous activities of listening and taking notes in a lecture can be very difficult if the lecture is fast paced. Unless you maintain some internal dialogue involving repetition of a critical phrase you wish to record, it is displaced by new information, and you quickly forget the important information.

If you are to minimize forgetting from short-term memory as you learn, you need to be very aware of situations that lead to overload and, whenever possible, apply strategies that will enhance storage into long-term memory. For example, reading a text commonly causes overload problems on your short-term memory. If you were to read many pages without pausing to apply strategies leading to long-term storage of the information, then the load on your short-term memory would increase to the point that you would forget much of what you had read.

Long-Term Memory

This is the component of memory that stores all the information an individual has learned. Much like a very large library or a computer with a 15-GB hard drive, it has an immense storage capacity. However, it also resembles a library in the sense that very careful storage and retrieval procedures are needed so that information is not lost inside the system. Unfortunately, many students do not have conscious and reliable procedures for information storage and retrieval. This results in forgetting information. The remainder of this chapter deals with strategies to enhance long-term storage of memories.

AN INTRODUCTION TO STRUCTURING INFORMATION

The way in which you critically select and structure new information to store in long-term memory is probably the most important contributing factor to your success as a student. If you are enjoying academic success, chances are that you are actively seeking out the main ideas and supporting details of your courses and structuring them around a set of interconnected themes. These structured memories facilitate efficient retrieval of the information at a later time.

The approach of less-successful students contrasts sharply with this. Typically, the less-successful student just tries to memorize lots and lots of facts, often with very little connection among the many facts that are being stored.

To get a sense of the power of information structuring, try the following exercise. Read the passage below as though you were going to have to remember it for a test.

> The procedure is actually quite simple. First you arrange things into different groups. Of course, one pile may be sufficient depending on how much there is to do. If you have to go somewhere else due to lack of facilities, that is the next step, otherwise you are pretty well set. It is important not to overdo things. That is, it is better to do too few things at once than too many. In the short run this may not seem important but complications can arise. A mistake can be expensive as well. At first the whole procedure will seem complicated. Soon, however, it will become just another fact of life. It is difficult to foresee any end to the necessity for this task in the immediate future, but one never can tell. After the procedure is completed one arranges the materials into different groups again. Then they can be put into their appropriate places. Eventually they will be used once more and the whole cycle will then have to be repeated. However, that is part of life.[3]

Most people report that when they first read this passage, it does not seem to make much sense, and it reads as a string of unrelated facts. Is this how you responded to it? If so, you would have found it difficult to memorize the information that it contains.

But wait! Give this passage a title, "Doing the Laundry." Now read it again and note what happens. The title helps you to structure the information as you read, and the passage makes a lot more sense. "Doing the Laundry" has retrieved from your long-term memory a relevant pattern of all the elements connected to this particular activity. This pattern includes a *purpose* for the activity (to launder clothes); necessary *component parts* (dirty clothes, detergent, washing machine); a *logical sequence of events* for the process (sorting and placing clothes in the washing machine, then drying, folding, and putting them away); and an end product or *conclusion* (clean clothes).

On rereading the passage with its title, you are able to structure the information into a meaningful big picture. Your short-term memory compares the ideas of this passage with the pattern for laundry that you retrieved from your long-term memory. Now, the information is easier to remember because you have mental images to attach it to.

---

[3] Bransford, J.D., & Johnson, M.K. (1992). Contextual prerequisites for understanding: Some investigations of comprehension and recall. *Journal of Verbal Learning and Verbal Behavior, 11,* 717–26.

Patterns of information that you have stored in your long-term memory are powerful aids to comprehension and memory. As a Good Strategy User, you need to be actively comparing any new incoming information with already-stored patterns. If the course material is very new to you and you do not have stored patterns to compare it to, you need to identify patterns within that course that you can use as a guide. This will not only help you to recognize and encode new information more readily, but it will also assist you in generating expectations about new information. You will be able to anticipate where your instructor is going with a topic.

So, how do you develop this skill of structuring new information by comparing it to patterns of academic information? First, you need to become aware of patterns of differences among academic disciplines. Second, you need to tune in to the hierarchical arrangement of headings and subheadings that identify the themes and subthemes that together make up the big picture. Third, you need to develop an active system for identifying the pattern of main ideas within an individual course.

LOOKING FOR PATTERNS AMONG DISCIPLINES

An instructor was talking with a group of new students and trying to help them with the transition to university learning. This instructor was an anthropologist, and she admitted to having a view of the world that was shaped by her discipline. She noted that the kinds of questions that were asked in her discipline, the methods of inquiry and reporting, and the vocabulary used were all specific to the discipline. As an anthropologist and an instructor, she was intent on educating students in her discipline. "When you walk through the door of my classroom," she said, "you must become an anthropologist. I want you to think, speak, research, and write like an anthropologist."

These students were being introduced to the idea that individual disciplines take a unique approach to their subject matter. Anthropology is different from chemistry, which, in turn, is different from classical studies, business, or nursing. Disciplines differ not just in subject matter but also in the methods of inquiry that produce and maintain the subject matter. This is not an easy idea to grasp, and many students who are starting out at a college or university make the mistake of treating all courses alike and taking exactly the same approach to each course. However, the Good Strategy User works at identifying the differences and similarities among disciplines and approaches each course in a way that is appropriate to it.

Think about the courses that you are currently taking and about the ways in which researchers have contributed to those disciplines. What makes them similar to or different from each other? For example, what methods of inquiry generated the knowledge, and what teaching methods are used to pass it on to you, the learner? What kinds of challenges does the subject matter pose to you as a learner? For the courses that you are currently taking, which two are most similar? In what ways are they similar? Which two of your current courses are most different, and what makes them so?

Two similar courses: _____ and _____

How they are similar:

_____

_____

Two contrasting courses: _____ and _____

How they are different:

_____

_____

TRACKING PATTERNS AMONG HEADINGS AND SUBHEADINGS

Most modern texts are highly structured. You are likely familiar with the typical layout of text chapters, each with a title and hierarchy of headings and subheadings. Main headings in the hierarchy are usually made to stand out by having the boldest and largest font. Second- and third-level headings are smaller and less dramatic, reflecting their relationship in the hierarchy of information. If you are an experienced Web surfer, you are likely familiar with the hierarchy of information that you explore through clicking onto a succession of URLs. This structured organization of information that you search on the Internet is just a longer reflection of the structure found in one academic text or lecture.

This pattern of headings and subheadings in a text can play a key role in how you store the information you are reading on a long-term basis. It provides you with the outline or superstructure around which you will eventually build relevant details. Imagine for a moment a very large building under construction: The first visible stage is the framework of steel girders that define the building's eventual size and shape. This steel framework guides all the components as the building is completed piece by piece. The hierarchy of headings in a text chapter acts much as the structural framework of the building by guiding you in adding important details one by one. Tuning into this hierarchy of headings while reading is the first step to structuring key ideas in memory. Look ahead to page 105 in Chapter 7, "Learning from Textbooks," for an example of a chapter outlined by a student.

Lectures are less predictable in presenting this hierarchical structure of ideas. In some classes, the instructor will begin with a lecture outline, so translating these main headings to your class notes does not require much effort. In other classes, however, the organizational pattern may be less obvious, and you will have to seek out the subthemes to the lecture and create your own set of headings.

If you want to improve your memory of texts and lectures, the next time you sit down to read a text chapter or take notes from a lecture, set yourself the goal of selecting and reinforcing in some way that hierarchy of headings and subheadings.

IDENTIFYING PATTERNS OF MAIN IDEAS IN A COURSE

Many students tell us that identifying the main ideas in a course is particularly problematic, whether they are learning information from a lecture, discussion in the classroom, or textbook or other reading materials. This is a really tough problem, both for the students and for the authors of this book. Because of the tremendous variety of courses and materials, it is not easy to come up with comprehensive categories of information that most commonly constitute the main ideas in a course. But we are presenting you with some ideas, and you can add to them if your courses go beyond these common patterns.

The following is a list of some generic types of "main ideas" that you will inevitably recognize from your courses:

- Key Terms and Their Definitions
- Academic Arguments
- Theories and Laws
- Relationships

These types of main ideas are not mutually exclusive (i.e., you may be able to place a main idea into several of the categories). Also, this list is not exhaustive, but it does cover types of information commonly found in a wide variety of courses. If information in a course that you are taking does not seem to fit into these categories, determine what kind of information it is and add to the list. As you get tuned into your courses and consistently seek out main ideas, you will begin to see some patterns emerging in the way in which information is presented. When you are familiar with these patterns, you will find that you can much more readily identify the main ideas that typically show up in tests and that also are the ideas that you will want to retain as part of your general knowledge base.

Let's now take a closer look at each of these categories.

Key Terms and Their Definitions

In any course, there are key terms describing the main ideas, and they are usually not hard to recognize. In a text, for example, they may be highlighted in a passage in **bold** face or *italic* type, constitute a subheading (as above), or may even be listed in a glossary at the end of the chapter. In a lecture, key terms will often be repeated by the instructor, emphasizing their importance, and they will often be displayed on an overhead or written on the chalkboard. Although key terms tend to stand out in these ways, it is still common for students to be unable to answer test questions based on them. Why should this happen if these key terms are relatively easy to identify?

The first problem is that many students do not recognize the importance of structuring information and, therefore, do not see these key terms as important. Second, many students suffer from the "I know that" syndrome when they are studying; they look at a term and think that they know it and don't need to put in any extra memory work to remember it. This cavalier attitude can lead to disappointing test results.

The key terms describe the central concepts, so watch out and listen for the way in which they are highlighted. In a well-structured course, they will be easy to find, but it might be a real challenge in a course with less organization. Make sure that you can define the key terms and know why they are so significant. Generating your own examples to illustrate the key terms can help anchor them in your long-term memory. Finally, find ways to self-test on the key terms. Retrieving these key terms or their definitions from memory as you learn will facilitate their retrieval during a test.

Academic Arguments

Academics and other researchers love to argue. In fact, the key goal of their work is to question aspects of the world around them, and academic debate is the central process for evaluating alternative answers to questions. Therefore, a great deal of academic information is in the form of persuasive arguments that attempt to explain the behaviour of people or things. For example, psychologists generate arguments to account for the behaviour of individuals; chemists debate about the behaviour of chemical substances in various states.

You are no doubt familiar with argumentative reasoning. On many occasions, you will have heard people supporting their positions on a variety of issues ranging from which hockey team will win the Stanley Cup to the best way to lower Canada's national debt. The only difference between this everyday form of debate and the academic variety is that the latter must be vigorously and rigorously evaluated.

Many test questions are based on remembering important elements of specific arguments or on applying the ideas of an argument to a new situation. Unfortunately, students may not realize that the main ideas within course material can be selected and structured very effectively based on the pattern of an academic argument. Therefore, they try to learn everything as unrelated details instead.

Patterns of Arguments

You need to be very familiar with the pattern of arguments. There are several common elements:

- What is the argument or issue under discussion?
- Are there any assumptions or premises that have been built into the argument?
- What type of evidence is put forward to support the argument?
- What conclusions are drawn from all the evidence?

Any one of these parts of an argument can come under intense scrutiny and even criticism by others. You should get into the habit of asking yourself questions about the arguments: "What is the issue here? How does this explanation compare to others on this same issue? Does this explanation provide a new insight into this issue?"

Theories and Laws

The ultimate goal for all academic arguments is to be able to find comprehensive explanations for complex phenomena and to simplify that complexity so that as many people as possible understand and can use the ideas. Theories and laws are explanations, often with relationships clearly specified. Usually, much effort—many studies, investigations, and great insight—has gone into developing theories and laws. Therefore, they are core material in almost every course, and students need to pay particular attention to them.

Theories and laws are usually not hard to find since they usually have the word theory or law attached to their name. For example, in sociology and other social science disciplines, we have Marx's conflict theory, and in physics, we have Boyle's gas law. While theories and laws may be relatively easy to identify, the main challenge for you, the learner, will be to tie all of the ideas together in long-term memory. What is the name of the theory or law? Whose name is pre-eminently linked to it? What was the seminal work that led to the insight? In the social sciences, can you relate the theory to modern examples? In the sciences, can you solve problems based on these ideas?

Relationships

One of the most fascinating classes of main ideas has to do with relationships. Questions on relationships—about how things interact or operate together—frequently show up in test questions. For example, you may be asked to explain the relationship of population density to urban structures in a geography test or to show how hours of daylight affect growth of corn in a plant sciences test. In science, you will learn about many chemical and physical reactions that can be described as formulas or graphs. The possibilities are endless when we begin to look at relationships in course material. However, because of their value as test questions, it is very important that you seek out and identify the main patterns of relationships that show up in your courses.

This list of relationships barely touches the tip of the iceberg in relationships that you should be watching for. However, each one is very common and will already be familiar to you.

- **Compare and Contrast:** similarities and differences among things.
- **Correlations:** ways in which a change in one variable is associated with a change in another.
- **Cause and Effect:** examination of underlying causes for events or phenomena.
- **Classes and Hierarchies:** organization of many items into a limited set of common categories that may be linked.
- **Systems:** an interacting set of parts working together for a unified purpose.
- **Threshold:** a critical point or value at which significant change occurs.

CONSOLIDATING INFORMATION IN LONG-TERM MEMORY

We have stressed the importance to memory of seeking out structure in the information you have to learn in your courses. However, forgetting is a fact of life, and time can erode much of what you have learned. As a Good Strategy User, what can you do to consolidate the information that you initially structured into long-term memory and thus avoid forgetting?

You can strengthen your memory through associations (encoding the information in a variety of ways) and through periodic review or rehearsal of the information. Current theories on memory suggest that when we forget, we mainly lose our connection to a thought, but we do not always lose the thought itself. If we want to retain as much information as possible, we have to make many connections so that if we lose one, there are still plenty of other connections to do the job.

As we look at strategies for association and rehearsal, it is important to keep in mind the end products of memory strategies. *Rote memory* implies memory with little regard for the meaning of the information. *Flexible memory* implies memory that not only is based primarily on the meaning of the information, but also on how to apply that information to different situations. Clearly, academic learning mainly requires strategies to enhance flexible memory.

Association Strategies

The following association strategies will enable you to consolidate information in long-term memory:

- Examples
- Visual Imagery
- Connections among Ideas
- Mnemonics

These strategies are highlighted individually because of their unique contributions to effective storage of information, but they are often used together.

Examples

Make up your own examples and, if appropriate, counter-examples of new topics that you are learning. A counter-example is something that would *not* illustrate a concept. This is especially useful in science. In an environmental chemistry course, for example, you might think of cleaning products used in the home that are acid in composition. Counter-examples would be those products that are basic and not acidic.

Often the most powerful associations are those that relate to your own personal experiences. This is easier to do in some courses—kinesiology, geography, psychology, and sociology—than it is in others. You will tend to remember personal examples in a meaningful and flexible manner.

Visual Imagery

Visual images are often very easy to remember, so try to create an image that captures the new topic you are learning. Images can be directly related to the new topic. For example, to illustrate your understanding of operant learning in psychology, you can *visualize* your dog bounding up to you for his "positive reinforcer" (dog biscuit). Visual images can also be based on analogies that are especially important to understanding complex and abstract concepts. For example, the simple geometric form of a pyramid can be used to describe the structure of a large business organization or government department. The flow of water in a river can help to explain the flow of electricity in an electronics course. An analogy acts as a model, the purpose of which is to simplify the complexity of real-world phenomena and thus enhance memory of that information.

The special power of visual imagery is that it enables the learner to transform abstract concepts into more concrete images. This is a well-known method for consolidating memory.

Connections among Ideas

In any one course, make connections among ideas presented in class and information from the text, lab, or tutorial. Also, relate together information from different courses, especially courses that build on each other in the same field. At times, you may have to check back to notes from previous courses to reactivate and reinforce essential basic concepts. Unless you can get a sense of the big picture, you will not be able to understand fully the individual concepts that are presented. The big-picture setting is essential to a sound and flexible memory.

Mnemonics

Mnemonics are memory devices that involve making arbitrary, but easy to remember, associations. They might involve colour, shapes, images, or anything that can be linked to the information you have to remember. Mnemonics do have one drawback: they do not involve meaningful associations, and so they should be used sparingly for very specific information that you are having trouble remembering. (Remember "Every Good Boy Deserves Fudge" from your music classes?)

However, mnemonics can be very powerful and allow you to recall detailed and complex ideas. Used appropriately, mnemonics are often essential for an optimal exam-review plan. There are specialized books on the market and even on the Internet on types of mnemonics, but the following are just a few of the most commonly used types:

- Rhymes
- Sounds
- Acronyms
- First Letters
- Loci

Rhymes

Rhymes are catchy and allow us to recite information that would be difficult as plain prose. If you enjoy playing with language, you might try making up some rhymes in your next test review. Rhymes do not have to be long to be effective. One student used the short and sweet mnemonic of "*Id* is the kid" to remember part of Freud's basic three-part theory about human personality.

Sounds

Somewhat like rhymes are simple sounds that can be tied to facts that you may find hard to remember. In a biology class on genetics, you will learn about the phenotype and genotype. How can you remember which is which? The sound of "fffff" can help you through association. The word phenotype begins with the "fffff" sound as do the words "face" and "photo." These words will remind you that "(fffff)enotype" is the visible expression of the genetic make-up (i.e., what you can see), just as you can see a face or a photo.

Acronyms

Acronyms are very special words. Each letter represents something of importance to remember. The term "sohcahtoa" is an easily remembered word that summarizes the important trigonometric definitions of sine, cosine, and tangent (sine equals opposite over hypotenuse, etc.). When you are learning your French verbs, you may come across the acronym of DR and MRS VANDERTRAMPP, an acronym representing the verbs in the past tense that are conjugated with *être* instead of with *avoir*.

First Letters

There are some types of information that are really difficult to remember without mnemonics. They might be drugs in a pharmacology class, bones and muscles in an anatomy class, or hormones in a physiology class. One way to memorize them is to generate a sentence in which the first letter of each word is the first letter of the item you have to remember (see the music example earlier). You might recognize this mnemonic from biology: Kings Play Chess On Frosted Glass Surfaces. This helps you to remember the relationships among Kingdom, Phylum, Class, Order, Family, Genus, and Species.

Loci

The Latin word *locus* means a place, so this mnemonic has to do with associating information with places. If you enjoy visual imagery, this mnemonic can be a lot of fun to create. There are many ways to interpret the loci mnemonic. Many memory books suggest creating mental images of items that you are trying to remember and associating them with different locations in your house. A somewhat different interpretation is illustrated by the following example that uses a hand-drawn map noting seven locations. Noted psychologist Albert Ellis theorized that the lives of many people are made difficult by irrational beliefs that they hold about life. Seven irrational beliefs, according to Ellis,[4] are as follows:

1. We should be *Loved* by absolutely everyone.
2. We should be *Competent* in all areas.
3. People who are *Wicked* should always be punished.
4. We should always try to *Avoid* difficulties.
5. Any *Past* event that was traumatic will always haunt us.
6. If things are *Not the way* we want them to be, then life is a disaster.
7. Problems that we face are *Externally* caused.

To use the loci mnemonic, for each belief, one word has been chosen as being able to encapsulate the idea, and the first letter has been capitalized. In Figure 5.2, a map of a familiar area was quickly hand drawn (in this case, southwestern Ontario). Seven locations were chosen that began with those seven first letters, and the place names have been placed on the map. The visual impact of the map allows relatively easy recall of those seven places. For the mnemonic to work well for you, choose an area that you know well. Enough memory work needs to be done to connect those seven letters to the seven ideas.

---

[4] Ellis, A. (1967). Rational-emotive psychotherapy. In D. Arbuckle (ed.), *Counseling and psychotherapy: An existential-humanistic view.* New York: McGraw-Hill.

FIGURE 5.2   AN APPLICATION OF THE LOCI MNEMONIC

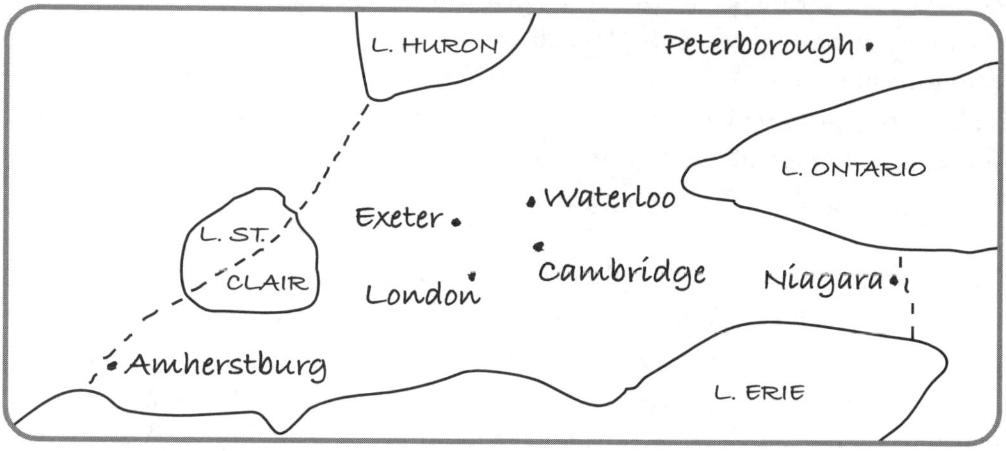

Rehearsal Strategies

Rehearsal strategies are extremely important for consolidating information in long-term memory because they give you practice doing what you will be doing on a test—retrieving information from long-term memory. In the time period immediately before a test, most of your study time should be spent using these rehearsal strategies:

- Recite Key Ideas
- Predict Questions
- Review Old Exams

Recite Key Ideas

Using headings as cues, try to recall the main ideas under each heading you have learned. This procedure is both simple and portable—you can do it almost anywhere (e.g., sitting on a bus or while washing the dishes). Also, if you have the opportunity, you might get other people involved by giving them your study notes and asking them to check how well you remember the content. Recitation trains retrieval processes and is especially important in preparing for multiple-choice exams where reliable memory of many concepts is emphasized. For problem-solving and essay exams, some recitation is necessary, but this must be balanced with application of ideas.

Predict Questions

In all courses, spend time predicting likely test questions for each topic. This can be done in a variety of ways:

- keeping the idea of patterns of ideas in mind and generating questions around those main ideas from your lecture notes and texts;
- checking out questions that are posed in your text or study guide;
- looking through homework questions that you were assigned and thinking how you could adapt them for the test; and
- sharing questions with others.

Review Old Exams

If available, old exams can provide you with excellent opportunities to rehearse writing real exams. As far as possible, simulate exam conditions by working in a quiet and undisturbed location. Avoid falling into the trap of looking up the answer right after trying a question, especially if you are having difficulty retrieving information from long-term memory. Before checking with your textbook or looking up the answer, give yourself time to activate a variety of retrieval cues. You may find that the required information will suddenly flash back into your short-term memory. This struggle to remember is good training for the real exam.

THE CRUCIAL ROLE OF COMPREHENSION MONITORING

As powerful as the ideas and strategies presented in this chapter might be, their effectiveness hinges on one crucial factor—comprehension monitoring. If course information does not make sense to you, you will not remember it, and, even if you do manage to memorize it, it is unlikely that your memory will be flexible enough to apply the ideas to new situations. That is why you need to monitor your level of comprehension. Use the symptoms listed in Box 5.1 as a checklist for your level of comprehension in one of your courses. Feel free to add, in the extra spaces, other symptoms that you experience.

BOX 5.1 COMPREHENSIVE MONITORING

NAME OF COURSE: _____

Cognitive Symptoms

_____ 1. In class, everything moves too fast for me.

_____ 2. There are so many details that I can't see any big picture.

(continued)

(continued)

_____ 3. I can't generate any examples on my own.
_____ 4. Even though I study a lot, I can't remember very much of this stuff.
_____ 5. I find it difficult to focus my attention when trying to learn this material.
_____ 6. This topic just doesn't make sense to me.
　　　　 7. _____
　　　　 8. _____

Emotional Symptoms

_____ 1. I have this gut feeling that I haven't really grasped this topic yet.
_____ 2. I feel overwhelmed, even scared, by the information.
_____ 3. I feel angry about having to learn this junk.
_____ 4. This stuff is so boring.
_____ 5. I am not at all confident of my ability to do this task.
_____ 6. I wish I were not taking this course.
　　　　 7. _____
　　　　 8. _____

PUTTING THESE IDEAS TO WORK

THIS CHAPTER BEGAN by introducing a model of memory systems. In particular, it encouraged you to think about the challenge presented to you by each one of the three components of memory. The major contribution of this chapter, though, is to emphasize the importance of structuring information as you learn. You are encouraged to seek out and recognize patterns in academic information. Establishing a soundly structured memory is a key goal to aim for. Once you have created a memory, you need to maintain it. Forgetting will happen, but your reinforcement of memories can maintain them longer and re-create them faster.

Your challenge at this point is to put these ideas into practice. It does not have to involve a drastic change to the way that you do things. Building more effective study habits can be done one small step at a time. However, powerful thinking strategies can make a real difference to your learning. These ideas will be reinforced for you as you read the next two chapters, "Learning from Lectures" and "Learning from Textbooks," which look at the key study tasks of learning from these sources.

CHAPTER 6

Learning from Lectures

LEARNING OBJECTIVES

The purpose of this chapter is for you to:

→ Identify ways that you can be a good listener.
→ Learn effective strategies for recording lecture notes.
→ Monitor your comprehension in lectures.
→ Learn about effective strategies to review lecture notes.
→ Learn a selection of abbreviation strategies.
→ Assess how to handle problem lectures.

WHAT IS YOUR experience with lectures? In this chapter, we ask you to think about some of your general strategies for lectures. As your instructor presents information, it is your responsibility to listen to and record the most important information that is presented. Since lectures are usually crucial components in your educational experience, you need to consider how you can make the most out of each one.

This chapter will introduce a variety of specific note-taking strategies that you can use to select and record the most relevant information from each lecture. It will also discuss how to prepare for lectures and how to review your notes at an appropriate time. As you read through this chapter, put a check mark by any strategy that you do *not* presently use. When you have finished the chapter, make a decision about which new strategies you will practise when you go to your next lecture.

INVENTORY OF LECTURE STRATEGIES

Consider the following ways of learning from lectures, and evaluate your strategy use by responding to each with either YES or NO.

1. I attend every (or almost every) lecture in each of my courses.
2. I prepare for class by reading, or at least scanning, the relevant parts of the text before going to the lecture.
3. I consult my course outline regularly so that I can see which topics we have completed and which we are about to cover.
4. I go to each lecture intending to learn as much as possible.
5. I sit in a location where I can see and hear easily.
6. I avoid external distractions in the lecture (e.g., chatty friends, sitting by the door where people are likely to enter late, etc.).
7. I try to control internal distractions such as worrying thoughts or daydreaming as I listen to the lecture.
8. I use abbreviations to capture the meaning of what the instructor is presenting rather than just copying down what is said.
9. I can listen and record at the same time competently.
10. If I get lost during a lecture, I work extra hard at trying to reconnect with the instructor rather than just giving up.

11. I work on making my notes meaningful and easy to read.
12. If I don't understand something in a lecture, I get help promptly.
13. I review and edit my notes soon after each lecture.
14. As I consolidate my notes after class, I look for and highlight the structure in the information.

Comment on your own experience with learning from lectures.

15. _____

16. _____

17. _____

18. _____

YOUR ROLE IN THE LECTURE

Identify the Purpose of Lectures for Each of Your Courses

Often lectures are the main source on which tests are based. Sometimes, however, the purpose of the lectures is to highlight important points in the text or to elaborate on printed notes that your instructor has distributed in hard copy or displayed on the course Web site. Still other lectures discuss readings or cases that you have to read before going to class. By knowing the purpose of your lectures, you can choose the best strategies for the course. For example, for lectures that highlight text or other written material, comprehensive note taking is not as crucial, but reading before the lecture is.

Try to Do as Much Learning During Lectures as Possible

As obvious as this seems, a careful look at the behaviour of many students in lectures indicates that they are not doing much learning. Some students talk to friends, read the newspaper, or stare off into space. Less obvious, but much more frequent, are the students who suffer from "stenographer's syndrome"—simply getting down everything that the instructor says or writes down, with little effort spent on thinking about what it means. For these students, minimal learning takes place in the lecture, and the notes that result are often not very useful. Avoid taking an ineffective role or a ho-hum attitude to lectures. Instead, go into class with a keen interest in both learning as much as possible and recording notes in a meaningful way.

Work on Developing Your Learning Strategies for Lectures

Most of the strategies presented in this chapter do not come to students naturally—they need to be developed. For example, the method of putting key words in the left margin is demonstrated in the next few pages. Done after the lecture, this is an excellent way of consolidating information into long-term memory.

LISTENING STRATEGIES

Aids to
Listening

Active listening will help you to get as much as possible from a lecture. Try the following:

Before

Before the Lecture

1. Survey or
   read ahead
2. Intend to
   listen

3. Location

4. Review
   previous

1. Survey or read ahead in the text before class in order to recognize new ideas and vocabulary.
2. Go to class intending to listen. Play an active role. It is your responsibility to find ways to stay interested in your lectures.
3. Select a place to sit in the classroom where you can keep your attention on the instructor and see and hear as well as possible.
4. Quickly review your notes from the previous class. This will help you to make connections with the previous lecture.

5. Check
outline

6. Mental
energy

5. Check the course outline regularly to keep track of the sequence of topics.

6. Manage your time so that you can go to class with as much mental energy to listen as possible. If you go to class tired, it will be difficult to concentrate.

During

1. Opening
statements

2. Instructor's
cues

3. Structure
material!

4. Own general
knowledge

5. Ask!

6. Lapses

During the Lecture

1. Listen for opening statements outlining topics, format, or philosophy.

2. Watch the instructor, and not the rest of the class. Spend some time really watching how the instructor emphasizes major points through voice, movements, pauses, etc. These cues will help you to discriminate between main ideas and supporting information.

3. Look at the way the instructor has organized the material. If it is not well structured, try to organize it for yourself. In particular, seek out the patterns that organize the ideas. Listen and watch for the main ideas.

4. Be aware of your general knowledge of the topic. Try to associate it with this new information to give it more meaning.

5. If you do not understand a point, ask for clarification (either during the lecture or after class).

6. Be aware that by the middle of the lecture your attention may lapse.

RECORDING STRATEGIES

Organizing Layout

Why Organize
Layout?

You can improve your learning efficiency if you focus on making your notes as organized and as meaningful as possible when you are in the lecture. This focus on organization and meaning has two benefits:

1. Learn more	1. You will learn far more in the lecture itself and have less to do on your own.
2. Easier to use	2. Your notes will be much easier to read, edit, and review after class.

Overall Organization of Notes

1. Binders

1. Rather than using a notebook, take lecture notes on paper that you can store in loose-leaf binders so that you can file away handouts, etc., with the relevant lecture.

2. #'s & date

2. Make sure that each page is numbered or identified with a date.

3. One side only

3. Write on only one side of the paper. You can then use the other side of the page to add information from the text, examples, or review questions.

4. Margin

4. Draw a 2" (5 cm) margin on your notepaper, and then use the margin to highlight main ideas when you review notes after class.

5. White space

5. Leave lots of white space so that you can add comments later. Also, the notes look better and are easier to review for a test.

Ways to Organize

Ways to Organize Information in Notes

1. Title

1. Give each lecture a title even if the instructor does not. Ask yourself the question, "What is this all about?" When you give your notes a title, you are labelling the overall theme of the lecture. This allows you to see the big picture and to evaluate the role of the individual parts.

2. Catch class outline

2. If your instructor puts up an outline for each lecture on the board or overhead before class, make sure to get there early so that you can copy this down and use it to guide your organization of notes.

3. Highlight heads, subh.

3. Highlight headings and subheadings throughout the lecture by using capitals and underlining. Otherwise, the notes look like paragraphs of prose in which little stands out.

4. Indents

5. Bullets or #'s, letters
6. Graphs, diagrams: LARGE & LABEL
7. Alternative techniques

4. Indent information under the related heading. This structuring of information organizes related ideas together in your notes and in your long-term memory.
5. Under headings and subheadings, list important details with bullets, numbers, or letters.
6. Make graphs and diagrams large enough to read easily, and label them well so that they will be meaningful to you later on.
7. Decide on alternative note-taking techniques for different kinds of material. For example, when ideas are compared, you can draw a line down the middle and collect the relevant details on each side. Another example would be branching flowcharts for step-by-step decision making.

MONITORING COMPREHENSION STRATEGIES

Do You Understand?

1. Emotional
2. Cognitive
If not, back to notes

As you listen to the lecture and take notes, try to evaluate whether or not you are understanding the ideas. Remember those strategies for monitoring comprehension in Chapter 5, "Effective Memory," which included both emotional and cognitive symptoms. This active process of monitoring your own learning process is crucial to effective learning. If you find the material difficult, it is essential to get back to your lecture notes as soon as possible after class.

REVIEW STRATEGIES FOR LECTURE NOTES

Review Notes Promptly!

Research indicates that individuals forget 60 percent of random information that they hear within 24 hours. Although lectures comprise meaningful information, it is still very likely that if you do not reread your notes promptly, you will forget a good portion of the lecture material.

Strategies

1. Regular
   time

2. Set objective
   • Key words,
     Brief
     summary

   • Review
     questions
3. Record issues
   for
   clarification
4. Personal
   reflections
5. Reread
   every 2 wks.

Talk to
instructor &
other students

AVOID
recopying!

Review Strategies

1. Find a regular time (fifteen to twenty minutes) within 24 hours of the lecture to go over the notes that you took in class.
2. Set an objective for rereading.
   • Key words in the margin can summarize main points. This chapter demonstrates this. In this case, almost every line of information on the right hand side of the page is summarized by a key word or phrase in the left margin. Another approach might be to summarize sections of the lecture with questions in the margin. You can then use these questions to test yourself. A brief summary of the whole lecture can be a useful review tool.
   • Making up two or three review questions at the end of each lecture can anticipate a test situation.
3. Record on the blank page opposite to the notes any issues that you need to clarify, and then follow up by getting help from the instructor.
4. Add any personal reflections or expansion on the topic on the blank page or in white space in your notes.
5. Reread key words every two weeks in order to refresh your memory on course content.

If you wish to share your ideas about a lecture with fellow students, it would be valuable to use a computer to complete these steps. You can learn a lot from such exchange and from hearing what approach they take. It is also invaluable to find out about the instructor's perspective on the course and about what approach he or she advises if you are having real difficulties. As you will encounter many different types of lectures, your role is to find the best way to take notes for each course.

Warning! Avoid recopying notes. It uses up a lot of study time and you do not learn much because you are not actively selecting and organizing.

USING ABBREVIATIONS

Many lectures in university and college move so quickly that it seems impossible to get everything down. Worse yet, instructors often talk and write nothing down, but you are still expected to learn and record the material in some way. How do you handle this situation? You need to develop a rich set of abbreviations that you can use constantly during the lectures. The goal is to capture the meaning of each important idea in a brief, yet accurate, manner. Not only do abbreviations allow you to get down much more information, they also force you to focus on the meaning of the material and not simply on the words or letters. By the same token, learning shorthand is not recommended because it focusses on sounds and not on meaning. The following are some abbreviation strategies:

- Symbols
- Short Abbreviations
- Longer Abbreviations
- Omit Words and Abbreviate

Symbols

Use symbols for relationships:

∴ therefore, thus, or so
∵ because, since
↑ increase
↓ decrease
= equal to, same as

∝ is related to, depends on
→ leads to, implies that
& or + and, in addition to
vs or cf compare, contrast, or versus

Short Abbreviations

Create and use short abbreviations for common terms:

definition = def.
example = eg.
evidence = evid.
input = inp.
function = fxn.

mechanism = mech.
problem solving = ps.
sociology = soc.
psychology = psych. or χ
with = <u>w</u>

Longer Abbreviations

Use just enough of a word to make it recognizable:

background = bkgd.   enough = enuf.
government = gov't.   important = imp.
behaviour = bhvr.

Omit Words and Abbreviate

Shorten long statements both by omitting many of the unimportant words and by abbreviating the important ideas.

Given a statement such as:

> Examples like these lead researchers to hypothesize that successful problem-solving behaviour depends more on the structure of the knowledge base rather than on the content of that knowledge base.

An effective abbreviation would be:

> eg's → to hypoth. that sucsfl PS bhvr. ∝ more on knowl. base <u>struct</u>. than on knowl. base <u>content</u>.

SUGGESTIONS FOR THE PROBLEM LECTURE

1. You are having difficulty understanding lecture material. Have you:
   - ☑ completed assigned reading before the lecture?
   - ☑ tried to identify the patterns in the information?
   - ☑ asked for help after defining as accurately as possible the idea that is difficult to understand?
2. You find you can't get everything down in your notes. Check whether:
   - ☑ you really need to record every detail;
   - ☑ other students share your impression (can you exchange notes to fill in gaps?); and
   - ☑ you can develop appropriate abbreviations.

3. You seem to take down the "wrong" information. Do you:
   ☑ use subheadings to highlight the main points?
   ☑ identify the important information using patterns to guide your selection of main ideas?
   ☑ talk to other students after class to check out their perceptions?
   ☑ consult any summary provided by the instructor (e.g., on the course Web site)?
   ☑ tape a lecture and listen again to the same material so that you can improve your original notes with this review? Though taping is not usually an efficient way to learn in lectures it can help you to find out what is missing in your notes.

4. You find that you haven't reread your notes after several weeks in class. Consider whether:
   ☑ the lecture notes are an important feature of the course and if not, focus more on listening to lectures;
   ☑ your notes are too disorganized due to lack of editing; and
   ☑ you can schedule review time into your weekly study plan.

5. After two or three weeks, you still cannot follow the instructor. You can't pick out what's important or where the lecture is going. Try to:
   ☑ attend another lecture section in addition to, or instead of, the one to which you are assigned;
   ☑ explain the problem to the instructor to see if he or she has any suggestions for you;
   ☑ ask another student in the course if you can see his or her notes from the last lecture;
   ☑ talk to other students after class about their perceptions; and
   ☑ tape a lecture and listen again to the same material so that you can improve your notes with this review.

AN EXAMPLE OF STRATEGIC NOTE TAKING

Figure 6.1 is a sample page of notes taken in a first-year university biology lecture by a Good Strategy User. In this lecture, the instructor presented information that was summarized into several key diagrams displayed on the overhead projector. In addition, a handout of the diagrams was given to each student in the class. The instructor did not write anything on the chalkboard. As a result of this lecture format, many students took almost no notes at all despite the fact that this

FIGURE 6.1   A SAMPLE PAGE OF LECTURE NOTES

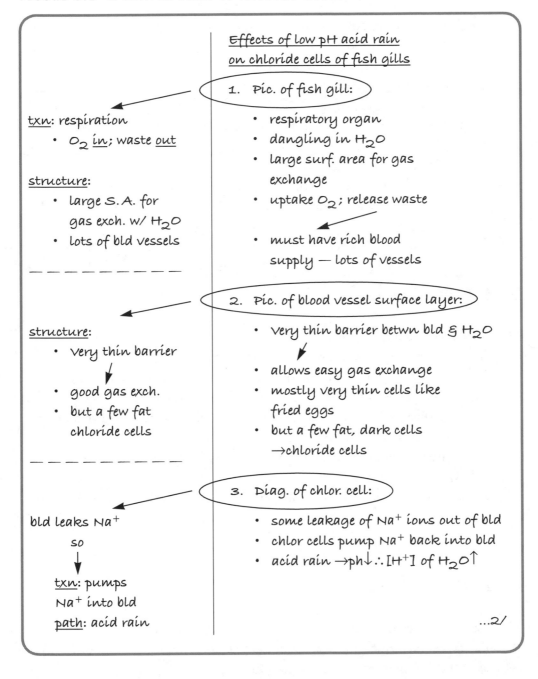

material was going to be on the next test and was not adequately covered in the text. So how did this Good Strategy User end up with both a good set of notes and a sound knowledge base of this material? Here are the note-taking strategies she used:

Before the Lecture

1. She checked the course outline to find out that the topic would be effects of low pH on the chloride cells of fish gills. She realized this topic was part of the unit on effects of acid rain on animals.
2. She thought about the kinds of relationships that would be stressed in this lecture (input, output, structure, function, mechanism, feedback control, and pathology). She was prepared to understand the harmful effects of acid rain on the chloride cells. (Note: She knew little about fish gills and nothing about chloride cells at this point.)
3. She drew a 2" (5 cm) margin on the left-hand side of her notepaper and prepared herself to write quite a bit, anticipating that this instructor would not write much.

During the Lecture

1. She stayed focussed on what the instructor was saying.
2. She used lots of abbreviations.
3. She tried to write down information that matched the relationships of a system. For example, at the beginning of the lecture, the instructor described function, position, and mechanism of the fish gill. She recorded this information in abbreviated form.
4. She organized her notes using headings, indenting, white space, and bullets.
5. She used the pauses in the lecture to go back and complete gaps in her notes.

After the Lecture

1. She spent fifteen minutes after class actively reviewing the notes by putting key words in the margin, relating her own class notes to the handout from class, and filling in missing information.
2. She was especially careful to make sure she understood both how fish gills worked as a system and how chloride cells worked as subsystem within the fish gill system.
3. She was not clear about the function of the chloride cells, so checked with the instructor.

WHAT ARE YOUR SUGGESTIONS?

Fatima's notes contain effective abbreviations and are a fairly concise record of lectures. In her astronomy course, she finds that her text overlaps with her lecture notes. She would like to combine the two sources of material. What would be the best way of doing this?

_____

_____

_____

Bill finds that he understands his business lecturer better if he listens carefully and does not attempt to take notes. On the weekend, he completes his record of the week's classes by using his text and remembering as much as he can. List the ways in which he can improve his record of this instructor's classes.

_____

_____

_____

Winnie is a conscientious student who takes careful, copious notes in all her lectures. Every two weeks, she rereads them and files them away until needed to review for exams. How can she improve her strategy in order to make better use of her notes?

_____

_____

_____

Not only does Majid find it difficult to get to his 8:00 A.M. lecture in sociology, but he can't take good notes from the instructor anyway. He decides to skip the lectures and work from his textbook instead. What comments would you make on this approach?

_____

_____

_____

THE KEY ROLE OF LECTURE NOTES

THIS CHAPTER HAS emphasized the crucial role that lecture notes take in your learning of course material. It is important, therefore, to find the most efficient set of strategies for taking notes. They should suit the course format, the role of the text or prepared outline and other learning resources, and your own learning style. Good notes will help you to identify prominent ideas, which you can then review within 24 hours of the lecture, periodically after that, and again just before a test.

This chapter has also identified alternative note-taking techniques and suggested ways to determine why you may not be satisfied with your notes. If you are having difficulty with learning from lectures, continue to attend class but talk to your instructor or a learning skills counsellor about the problem. Learning from lectures has much in common with the topic of the next chapter, "Learning from Textbooks," as both chapters focus on strategies for acquiring information. As you read the next chapter, think about the methods that are common to both situations.

CHAPTER 7

Learning from Textbooks

LEARNING OBJECTIUES

The purpose of this chapter is for you to:

➜ Assess your current reading strategies.
➜ Choose a reading approach that matches your reading demands.
➜ Consider reading strategies for prereading, reading comprehension, and post-reading activities.

THIS CHAPTER LOOKS at one of the most important things that students have to do—reading texts. When asked the question, "How much reading do you do for pleasure?" many students reply, "Not much." For these students, the amount of reading that is commonly demanded in post-secondary education can represent a daunting task. Whether or not you have had a lot of experience with reading in the past, this chapter suggests many reading strategies that can help you improve on your reading skills.

This chapter asks you to look first at the way you read academic texts. Then it stresses the importance of getting to know your texts before diving into your reading tasks. You will need to decide on an approach to reading that best matches the reading demands of your courses. Strategies for effective reading are presented for you to think about and choose among, since you are the one who will decide which are best for you.

WHAT IS A TEXTBOOK?

As there can be many different types of reading materials in academic courses, it is important to define what we mean by a textbook. However, that is not easy. It is almost simpler to list items that are not textbooks and are, therefore, not covered in this chapter. For example, novels, plays, and poems in an English course are not textbooks, nor are government documents and research articles. Although some of the reading methods suggested in this chapter may apply in some instances with such reading materials, they often need approaches more specific to their style and beyond the scope of this chapter.

A common characteristic of many texts is that they are organized into topics and subtopics. This careful structuring is highlighted by subheadings throughout. Some texts lack overt structure and look more like novels, making them more difficult to read. However, in many subject areas such as psychology, geography, and biology, the texts are generally carefully designed to facilitate the reading process for students. It is these structured texts that are the main focus of this chapter.

ASSESSING HOW YOU CURRENTLY READ

Before you evaluate the suggested reading strategies in this chapter with the goal of building new ways of reading, take time to reflect on how you currently read and, in particular, anything that facilitates or hinders your reading. Keep these issues in mind as you complete the self-assessment on how you currently read.

Of all the courses that you are currently taking, which is your heaviest reading course?

Name of course: _____

Think about this course for a moment, and, in particular, think about the last time that you were reading the textbook. What are three of the problems that you were dealing with?

1. _____

2. _____

3. _____

Now, with this course in mind, complete the following inventory by checking as many of the statements as you feel represent how you currently go about reading. As you check off each item, think about how satisfied you are with the way you are reading. Are there changes that you need to make? If the strategies that you use are not listed, add them in the spaces provided.

1. Time Management

_____ Every week, I regularly read the required pages.
_____ Periodically, I catch up by reading several chapters.
_____ I read the text only when I am reviewing for a test.
_____ I never (or rarely) read the text.
_____ I read some of the chapter but don't usually finish it.

_____

_____

2. Approach

_____ For any chapter, I just begin at the first page and read the chapter straight through.
_____ I spend some time looking through the chapter before beginning to read.
_____ I read the summary before I read the chapter.

_____   After I've finished reading the chapter, I spend some time looking over the headings again.

_____

_____

3. Integration with the Lecture

_____   I read the chapter before the topic is covered in class.
_____   I read the chapter after the topic is covered in class.
_____   Sometimes I read the chapter before and sometimes after the class.
_____   I check my class notes against the text.

_____

_____

4. Concentration

_____   I read where I won't be disturbed.
_____   I often spend three or four hours reading without taking a break.
_____   I take regular breaks after every hour or so.
_____   I have a definite goal in mind about what I want to accomplish, and I work toward it.
_____   I daydream a lot while I read.
_____   I allow myself to be easily distracted while I am reading.

_____

_____

5. Memory

_____   I just read and try to remember.
_____   I highlight.
_____   I take notes from the chapter.
_____   I use the study guide to reinforce the chapter.
_____   I recite aloud or to myself to memorize important points.

_____

_____

6. Exam Review

_____ I reread everything for every test.
_____ I reread my highlighting and/or my own summary notes.
_____ I reread the text summary.
_____ I use the study guide.
_____ I ask the instructor or other students about things I don't understand.

_____

_____

THE ROLE OF THE TEXT IN THE COURSE

There are a number of important questions that you need to ask yourself about the role of the text in any course that you take. As a Good Strategy User, the answers to these questions will direct the reading strategies that you select and use.

The first question is: "How important is this assigned text to my learning the content of this particular course?" Often, an instructor will talk about the text at the beginning of the course or discuss it in the course outline. Some instructors structure the entire course around the text, while others use it merely as a supplement. You will need to evaluate whether or not the text is viewed as a primary source from which you are required to learn detailed information or as reference material that can help you to solve problems as necessary.

A second question that will influence the way you read is: "How much reading is expected in this course each week?" If you are expected to read only 30 pages each week, then you can afford to spend time consolidating every detail. But if you are expected to read 300 pages, you will have to find ways to be very efficient. With so much to read, you will have to be much more selective about the material.

Lastly, ask yourself: "How will I be tested in this course, and how does the text fit with what I think will be on the exam?" If you are to be tested through detailed multiple-choice test questions drawn from the text, you will need to know _all_ the main ideas and important related details. But if you are to be tested through essay questions, you will need to be aware of major themes and _some_ of the key related ideas. It will also be beneficial to predict possible test questions.

Some students do not realize what role the text plays in each course and spend hours working on tasks that may not lead to success.

Nick's Dilemma

Nick had failed a psychology test. He was very upset and angry, and he threw a thick wad of notes taken from the text onto his desk.

"I really studied for that test," he said. "I put in hours of work, made all these notes, and my mark was 40 percent, a failing grade well below the class average."

As the above scenario illustrates, Nick had worked hard, putting in many hours with the textbook, but the other side of this story was that he did not like 8:30 A.M. classes and had attended few of the lectures in the course. The text covered only a small part of the course content—something that Nick had not realized. Therefore, despite hours spent reading his textbook, Nick was not very well prepared for the test. By carefully considering the role of the text in a course, you can avoid making the same mistake as Nick.

Avoiding Nick's Dilemma

Think about the role of the text in one of your courses. Identify the course and answer the following questions.

Name of course: _____

1. What messages has the instructor given about the way in which the text is to be used in the course?

   _____

   _____

   _____

2. How similar or dissimilar is the content of the lectures and text?

   _____

   _____

_____

_____

3. How important is the text to doing well on the examinations?

_____

_____

_____

4. What strategies are you currently using as you're reading this text?

_____

_____

_____

GETTING TO KNOW THE TEXT

When you begin a new course, spend some time browsing through the text before your first reading assignment to find out about the book's background, content, and organization. Getting to know the text before you begin reading can establish expectations that can affect reading strategies and comprehension of the material in a positive way. As you examine the text, take the following into consideration:

- Background
- Content and Organization of the Text as a Whole
- Content and Organization of Each Chapter

Background

The preface will often give you the answers to the following important background questions:

- Who Wrote the Text?
- When Was the Text Written?
- Where Was the Text Written?

Who Wrote the Text?

A text can be written by one or several authors. You may expect a more consistent style of writing if the text is written by one author than if written by several authors. Differing styles across the chapters may pose a challenge, and you may have to adjust your approach to reading to take this into consideration. It is also important to ascertain what information is given about the author and how the author's perspective affects the content.

In many disciplines, there are differing viewpoints on important issues. For example, you would expect a political commentary from a conservative author to contrast sharply with one from a liberal author. It is important for you to be alert to any possible bias on the part of the author before reading the text.

When Was the Text Written?

Many elements of our modern world are changing so rapidly that information and perspectives quickly become outdated. Always check the date of the publication to assess the relevance of the content. Of course, relevance will depend on the context within which you wish to use the information and the type of information in the textbook. For example, books about computers and other high-tech subjects are often obsolete soon after they are published, but history or geography texts have a longer life.

Where Was the Text Written?

The cultural environment within which the author was educated will have played an important role in the development of his or her ideas. There may have been important individuals or groups of people who strongly influenced the author's ideas, and the book may be putting forward one distinct perspective. As ideas change over time and from place to place, it is useful to know the context in which the ideas were formulated. The place and date of writing are often noted in the preface and on the copyright page.

Content and Organization of the Text as a Whole

Look through the table of contents at the front of the text and check the titles of all of the chapters:

- What topics are covered and in what order?
- What is the logic behind that particular order of topics?
- Is the book subdivided into major sections or parts?
- What additional information is included: preface, glossary, appendix, index?
- How do the topics in the text match the topics in lectures?

Ask yourself, "What do I already know about these topics? From my own experience, can I identify with any of these topics? Do I find them interesting, provocative, depressing?"

Look through your text and check off items as you identify them:

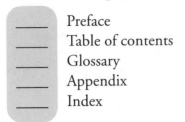

_____ Preface
_____ Table of contents
_____ Glossary
_____ Appendix
_____ Index

Content and Organization of Each Chapter

- How are the chapters organized? Are they subdivided into sections with subheadings, and, if so, can the sections be easily identified?
- What illustrative materials are employed: pictures, figures, tables?
- How are key ideas and definitions highlighted: bold text or italics?
- Is there a glossary of key words?
- Are questions posed to get the reader thinking?

Look through your text and check off items as you identify them:

_____ Learning objectives for each chapter
_____ Introduction and outline for each chapter
_____ Headings within each chapter
_____ Figures, tables, illustrations, etc.
_____ Conclusion or summary for each chapter
_____ Glossary for each chapter or at end of text
_____ Questions or problems based on each chapter

How does the chapter you are about to read link with those immediately before and after it? Each chapter will make more sense when viewed in the context of the big picture.

DECIDING HOW TO READ

It is very important that you realize that you should read different books in different ways. You are in charge of your own reading goals and you will need to decide how to read each varied assignment. The following questions will help you in your decision making:

- How many pages do I have to read?
- How much time do I have to read this material?
- What is the best time and place for me to do this reading in order to maintain concentration and complete the task efficiently?
- What other high-priority tasks are in competition for the available time?
- Am I going to be tested on this material, and, if so, how much detail will I have to know?
- How can I reinforce this information in my memory (highlight the text, marginal notes in the text, additional summary notes, the study guide, etc.)?
- How can I best organize myself so that I can work at this task in the most efficient way?

Two critical decisions that you must make about reading the text have to do with time management: when and where will you read? Ideally, you should read the text before each class so that you are as well prepared as possible for the lecture. There may be times when you are not able to do this, but it is certainly a goal to work toward. Regular reading and periodic review leads to much better test results than does cramming by reading several chapters for the first time just before a test.

Where you read is also a critical decision because the more you concentrate while reading, the "deeper" you will process the ideas, and the more you will remember. If you find a good location in which to read, you will find that you are spending less time on your reading assignments and remember the main ideas better.

READING STRATEGIES

As a Good Strategy User, you will not use all the reading strategies suggested in this chapter—only those that are appropriate to the project at hand. As you read and think about each method, evaluate it for its potential usefulness for your specific reading assignments. These strategies naturally fall into three groups:

- Prereading
- Reading for Comprehension
- Post-Reading

Prereading

The prereading stage should take only a few minutes and should accomplish the following:

- Activate Your Background Knowledge
- Survey Important Information
- Make the Outline of the Chapter into a Useful Review Tool

Activate Your Background Knowledge

Look at the chapter title and think about the theme of the chapter. What do you know about this topic? Recall relevant information. In particular, look through lecture notes if this topic has already been covered in class.

Survey Important Information

The following will give you important information about the chapter:

- the chapter title (what is the chapter about?);
- headings and subheadings (what are the main topics and how are they organized?);
- the introduction and summary (what do they highlight?);
- captions (what is illustrated in the pictures, figures, and tables?); and
- the bibliography (what are the additional materials on this topic?).

Make the Outline of the Chapter into a Useful Review Tool

On the title page for each chapter, some texts provide you with an outline of at least the main headings for the chapter. As already noted, you should survey these before reading in depth. You may even wish to photocopy each title page with its outline and staple all of the title pages together. These outlines make very useful review tools because you can look at the headings and subheadings on the outline and recall important points from memory.

If a chapter outline is not provided, you can make one for yourself. Writing all the headings and subheadings down will help you to begin to structure the information into long-term memory.

On a piece of paper or on your computer, first record the title of the chapter you are about to read, then scan through all the headings and subheadings, identifying the hierarchy of the different levels of headings. The main headings usually stand out by being larger or in a different colour. Make a list of all the headings and subheadings in that chapter, and highlight the hierarchy by indenting lower levels of headings so that the higher levels stand out. Paying attention to the hierarchy of headings is important to understanding how various ideas fit together.

Look at the example[5] in Box 7.2 and notice how the outline retains the relationship between the main headings and the subheadings.

Reading for Comprehension

When you read for comprehension, you should do the following:

- Identify Your Reading Units
- Pay Attention to Subheadings
- Pick Up Clues from the Text Layout
- Build the Big Picture
- Form Visual Images
- Read for Main Ideas
- Rephrase What You Read into Your Own Words
- Monitor Your Emotional Response to the Text
- Choose How You Will Make a Record of Key Information

Identify Your Reading Units

Make a decision about how much you will read for comprehension before beginning to use memory techniques such as underlining or highlighting key information. Several factors will influence your decision here: level of difficulty, number of pages to be read, and the level of detail that you are expected to retain. If the material is difficult for you or if it contains detailed new concepts, you may want to read one paragraph only before stopping to absorb the information. If, however, it is lighter, you can read several pages or even the whole chapter and then process it through highlighting, underlining, or summary notes.

If you have a large number of pages to read, you will have some hard decisions to make. If you are to be tested through essay questions, you may be able to move along at a fairly rapid pace and stop only occasionally to make brief summaries around important themes. However, if you are expected to have full and detailed knowledge of the information as required for multiple-choice tests, you will have to allot a number of hours on a regular basis to be able to go through it more thoroughly.

---

[5] The example is based on Chapter 6, "Religion," by Reginald W. Bibby, in the introductory text: Brym, Robert J. (1998). *New society: Sociology for the 21st century* (2nd ed.). Toronto: Harcourt Brace.

BOX 7.2 CHAPTER OUTLINE SHEET

Chapter 6 — Religion

1. Introduction

2. Sociology and Religion

3. Theoretical Traditions
   - Marx and Conflict
   - Durkheim and Collectivity
   - Weber and Ideas

4. The Nature of Religion
   - Personal Religiosity
   - Collective Religiosity
     - The Church–Sect Typology
     - Organizational Approaches
       * Membership
       * Goals
       * Norms, Roles, and Sanctions
       * Success
     - The Canadian Situation

5. The Sources of Religion
   - Individual-Centred Explanations
     - Reflection
     - Socialization
     - Deprivation
   - Structure-Centred Explanations

6. The Consequences of Religion
   - Personal Consequences
   - Interpersonal Consequences
   - Societal Consequences

7. The Future of Religion

Reminder: This list includes only the headings and subheadings used by the author in this chapter.

Pay Attention to Subheadings

As you begin to read each subsection of the chapter, focus on the subheading, and ask yourself what the section is about. Some subheadings clearly indicate what the focus of the section is, while others are less descriptive. Try to anticipate what information you will be reading.

Pick Up Clues from the Text Layout

In addition to subheadings, there are other clues to key ideas. If a word is highlighted in **bold** or *italicized* type, it is being emphasized, and you should evaluate it carefully. In addition, illustrative material (e.g., charts, graphs, figures, and tables) clarifies important concepts. Also, information inserted as a marginal note or as a box is there for a purpose. Look at it carefully to see what special contribution it makes.

Build the Big Picture

The title of a chapter specifies the overall theme, while the subheadings identify the contributing sections. You will be integrating relevant information into a big picture if you can keep your general knowledge and the lecture material in mind as you read. The more connections you make between each section of new information and your own general knowledge, the better you will understand and remember that information. The most powerful associations you can make are with your own experiences.

Form Visual Images

There are many topics that bring visual images to mind as you read. For example, in the outline of the sociology chapter on the previous page, the term "personal religiosity" can trigger thoughts and images about your own religious experiences. There is a lot of evidence to suggest that we remember visual images much better than we remember more abstract ideas. As you read, try to *see* the information, generating your own examples to illustrate the concepts.

Read for Main Ideas

Students report that reducing information to main ideas is one of their greatest difficulties when reading academic texts. There is always a risk that you will miss an important point when you try to select main ideas rather than learning absolutely everything. However, it is essential that you try to discriminate between key ideas and supporting details. As we discussed in Chapter 5, "Effective Memory," memory gets overloaded when a student tries to merely collect rather than structure information. Comprehension and good memory require that the student see the relationships among the various ideas presented and build a structured framework of the facts. Reread pages 62–69 on structuring information so that you can read effectively, looking out for the pattern of main ideas in your reading assignments.

Rephrase What You Read into Your Own Words

As you finish reading a paragraph, get into the habit of asking yourself the questions: "What was that all about?" and "What are the main ideas here?" If you can paraphrase the text into your own words as you read, you will be achieving two important goals:

1. You will be ensuring that you understand the information.
2. You will be striving to put that information into your long-term memory.

Monitor Your Emotional Response to the Text

Try to maintain a positive attitude toward the text as you read. Attitude is an important part of being a Good Strategy User and can have a strong influence on your ability to comprehend and assimilate key information. If you enjoy reading and get excited or fascinated by your new knowledge, you are more likely to remember that information. However, if you reject the ideas or feel bored, anxious, or irritated by the text, it will be more difficult for you to apply the ideas to tests or assignments.

Choose How You Will Make a Record of Key Information

The majority of students remember information better after highlighting or writing it down, and you should plan to record significant ideas this way. You can handwrite your notes or use your computer. Choose the method that works best for you and for a particular assignment. You may well find that you approach each reading task in a different way, the way that best matches that task. Consider the following effective strategies:

- Underline/Highlight to Facilitate Later Review
- Add Key Words/Brief Notes to the Margin of the Text
- Make a Separate Set of Summary Notes
- Develop a Diagram to Illustrate the Main Ideas and Relationships among Them
- Make Up Test Questions
- List Key Words

Underline/Highlight to Facilitate Later Review

If you read for understanding first and then go back to underline or highlight key ideas, you will have more success in choosing only the important points. Do not highlight too much text; instead, concentrate on the main idea in each separate paragraph. Use symbols such as brackets, boxes, asterisks, and circles to highlight different kinds of information. Also, if there is a sequence of facts in the information, number the points in order right in the text.

Add Key Words/Brief Notes to the Margin of the Text

Focus only on the main ideas for these key words and marginal notes. As you read, aim to structure information into a meaningful framework that highlights the relationships among the various ideas. In particular, look for the pattern of main ideas in that text.

Make a Separate Set of Summary Notes

In addition to being an aid to memory, condensed notes save time when it comes to reviewing for tests as well as reduce "interference" problems that can occur when too much information is processed over too short a time period. As much as possible, put the summary points into your own words, and avoid the common mistake of taking too many notes. This takes too long and does little to help you remember the information, so to avoid this, read at least a page before summarizing.

Many students end up with a great set of notes on paper but with very little knowledge in their long-term memory. You have to take the time to learn what is in your notes and not just the time to make them.

Develop a Diagram to Illustrate the Main Ideas and Relationships among Them

For many students, the more graphically the information is displayed, the easier it is to remember. This method is sometimes referred to as cognitive mapping.

Make Up Test Questions

If you can transform a chapter into a set of questions, you may be anticipating test questions. Trading the questions that you generate with a friend can help you both.

List Key Words

After reading a chapter, make your own glossary of the most important words. Make sure that you understand their meanings and can relate them to the broader context of the chapter. Understanding how crucial components contribute to the big picture is essential to academic success.

Note that both the highlighted text with marginal notes (Figure 7.1) and the summary notes (Figure 7.2) that follow focus only on the most important points made by the author. The Good Strategy User looks for patterns of main ideas to describe the structural framework of this important information.

FIGURE 7.1 AN EXAMPLE OF HIGHLIGHTED TEXT WITH MARGINAL NOTES

▲ COLLECTIVE RELIGIOSITY

[Marginal note: Group is important]

It is frequently argued that one can be religious without having anything to do with religious organizations such as churches or synagogues. However, most social scientists, beginning with Durkheim, would maintain that personal religiosity is highly dependent on **collective religiosity**, or group support of some kind. Such dependence is not unique to religion. It stems, rather, from a basic fact of life: The ideas we hold tend to come from our interaction with other people. However creative we might like to think we are, the fact is that most of the ideas we have can be traced to the people with whom we have been in contact — family, friends, teachers, authors. Moreover, if we are to retain our ideas, they must continuously be endorsed by at least a few other people. In modern societies where religious ideas compete with a wide variety of other ideas, it is essential for the maintenance of religion that religious groups exist to transmit and sustain religious ideas.

[Marginal note: Again – Group is key]

The Church–Sect Typology

Those who have examined religious groups in predominantly Christian settings have recognized two major kinds of organizations. First, there are numerically dominant groupings — the Roman Catholic Church in medieval Europe, the Church of England, the so-called mainline denominations in Canada and the United States (Anglican, United, Presbyterian, Lutheran), and so on. Second, smaller groups have broken away from the dominant bodies. For example, in the sixteenth century, "protestant" groups including the Church of England broke away from the Roman Catholic Church; but Methodists in turn broke away from the Church of England, and the Salvation Army emerged as a breakaway group from the Methodists. Today, additional "emerging" groups include an array of Baptist and Pentecostal denominations and congregations that are found in virtually every North American city.

[Marginal note: 2 types of groups]

[Marginal note: Mainline & Break away]

[Marginal note: New emerging groups]

From this pattern of dominant groups and breakaway groups, sociologists who are trying to make sense of religious groups developed an analytical scheme known as the **church–sect typology**. This framework attempted to describe the central characteristics of these two types of organizations, as well as account for the origin and development of sects.

[Marginal note: Analysis of Religion]

In perhaps its earliest formulation, Max Weber distinguished between church and sect primarily on the basis of theology (churches emphasize works, sects stress faith) and relationship to society (for

[Marginal note: Weber had two focuses: theology & relationship to society]

churches, accommodation; for sects, separation). Weber noted the irony in the sect's development: initially a spinoff from an established church, the sect gradually evolves into a church itself (Gerth and Mills, 1958). The sect is at first characterized by spontaneity and enthusiasm. In time, however, these traits give way to routinization and institutionalization.

Although the church–sect typology has been used extensively, alternative ways of understanding religious groups are now becoming popular.

Organizational Approaches

In sociological terms, religious organizations are no different from other social organizations. Therefore, there has been a growing tendency to analyze religious groups by making use of the same frameworks we use in studying social organizations in general. For example, from an organizational point of view, religious groups in Canada are in effect corporations of different sizes. The Roman Catholic Church is "a multinational corporation," the United Church is a company that is "Canadian-owned and -operated," the Baptist Union of Western Canada is "a regional company" with links to other "regional companies" in central and eastern Canada, and an individual congregation in a given city or town is "a local outlet."

[Marginal note: Comparison with Corporations]

Apart from provocative marketing language and corporate analogies, a general organizational approach to religious groups might lead us to examine them in terms of some basic features, including (1) the nature and the sources of their members, (2) their formal and informal goals, (3) the norms and roles that are established to accomplish their purposes, (4) the sanctions that are used to ensure that norms are followed and roles are played, and (5) the success that groups experience in pursuing their goals.

[Marginal note: 5 features members goals norms sanctions success]

MEMBERSHIP When one studies the membership of Protestant churches, one immediately notices that many members have parents who are involved as well. A 1994 national survey of the United Church of Canada, for example, found that about 70 percent of active members acknowledged that their mother or father had been United Church members (Bibby, 1994). Surveys of Anglicans, Roman Catholics, and members of evangelical churches — referred to as conservative Protestant groups by sociologists — have uncovered the same intergenerational pattern. As a result, new additions to almost any given congregation are primarily active members who are on the move geographically. By the same token, one of the major reasons for a decline in participation is the simple fact that people make

[Marginal note: Members Family Connection]

FIGURE 7.2   AN EXAMPLE OF SUMMARY NOTES

Collective Religiosity

- The group is the key to personal religiosity and to maintenance of religious groups

* The Church-Sect Typology
  Study of Christian groups shows:
  1. Large dominant (mainline) denominations
  2. Smaller breakaways from above # 1
  3. New emerging groups
- The church-sect typology describes central characteristics
  e.g., Weber looked at a) theology
                         b) link with Society

* Organizational Approaches
- Religions are social organizations similar to corporations
- Basic features
  ① Members
  ② Goals
  ③ Norms
  ④ Sanctions
  ⑤ Successes

  ① Members
    - Common to follow parents' example
    - New church members mainly people who have moved house
    - May stop attending church when move house

Post-Reading

The purpose of post-reading is to accomplish the following:

- Review Chapters
- Recite the Important Information from Memory
- Self-Test

Review Chapters

Forgetting will be a problem if there is a long gap between learning and testing.

☑ The first review should immediately follow the first reading. This should not take long because the information is still fresh in your memory.

☑ Try to find time every two weeks or so to engage in a quick review of the chapters. This will keep previously learned information fresh in your memory as the amount increases. This is especially important in subjects like math and science where material learned is cumulative.

☑ Before a test, plan a specific amount of time to spend in careful, thorough review.

Recite the Important Information from Memory

This is an important step in transferring information from short-term to long-term memory and then maintaining the information in long-term storage so that it is easily retrieved.

☑ Cover the page. Recite silently or out loud the important points that you need to remember. If you cannot remember, recheck the page and try again.

☑ You do not need to have the text or your summary notes on hand when you practise recitation. When you have some spare time (at the bus stop or changing classes), try to recall the organization of a chapter by reciting the subheadings.

☑ Think about the key word list or glossary that you prepared. How many of those words can you recall? Can you define them and give examples?

Self-Test

Monitor your levels of comprehension and memory through self-testing.

☑ Use scrap paper or your computer to record critical information from memory.

☑ Make up your own test questions, and use them to test yourself at a later date.

☑ If your text poses questions, make sure that you can answer them from memory.

☑ Recheck any concepts highlighted in the text in **bold** or *italics,* and make sure that you can define the terms and explain how they fit into the big picture.

☑ If old exams are available, rehearse by simulating the real test. Give yourself a time limit and answer the questions as though you were writing a real test.

☑ Organize or join a study group with a few classmates, and find ways to test each other.

☑ If your text has a study guide, answer questions in it.

TEXTBOOK TROUBLES

Lee has been busy his first month of school with classes, residence parties, and the fitness class he joined. He hasn't had time to buy all his textbooks yet, and he is already short of cash. So, he relies on borrowing his friends' books when necessary. What are the disadvantages of this?

_____

_____

_____

Julie is a really serious student who reads each chapter. She always makes summary notes but wonders if this is the best use of her time. What suggestions can you offer?

_____

_____

_____

Ling has a lot of course reading in her program. She makes herself sit down to read at least three hours each evening, one evening per course. Despite all this preparation, she does not join in class discussion because she cannot remember what she has read. Any suggestions?

_____

_____

_____

Alain does not like reading. He finds that he gets sleepy and loses his concentration within about fifteen minutes. How can Alain maintain a better concentration level?

_____

_____

_____

A PERSONALIZED APPROACH TO READING

YOU WILL NO doubt find that the knowledge you acquire from texts plays a vital role in your academic success. It is, therefore, essential that you find a way to read texts that is both manageable and effective for *each* of your courses. One of the mistakes that many students make is to read every text in exactly the same way. To avoid making that mistake, you first need to question the role of the text in each of your courses. Your reading assignments can vary greatly in the amount of time required and in the amount of detail that you expect to retain after reading. As a Good Strategy User, you will tailor the way you read a text to match its specific demands.

For any reading assignment, however, it is useful to consider planning your reading strategies around the same three stages in the reading process that this chapter has described: prereading, reading for comprehension, and post-reading. Which strategies you apply at each stage will depend on the task at hand. Your comprehension and retention of the information and your ability to apply what you have learned will be greatly enhanced if you work through these three stages in the reading process. The next chapter, "Problem Solving in Science and Engineering," focusses on science, and, as you read, you can think about how effective reading strategies are linked to both solving scientific problems and to completing your lab assignments successfully.

CHAPTER 8

Problem Solving in Science and Engineering

LEARNING OBJECTIVES

The purpose of this chapter is for you to:

→ Learn how to solve your problems efficiently.
→ Learn how to make better use of the resources and study time available to you.
→ Learn strategies for understanding concepts quickly and solving problems confidently.
→ Learn strategies for the efficient and successful completion of laboratory work.

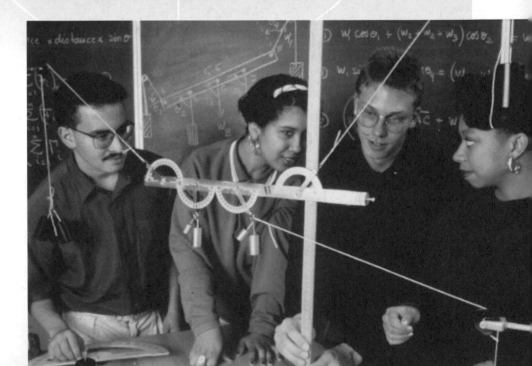

W HY DO SOME students do well in science and engineering problem-solving courses such as math, physics, and statistics, while others do poorly? Natural ability accounts for some of this difference, but strategies that students use are also very important in successful problem-solving performance. A science or engineering student who is a Good Strategy User makes use of the two different kinds of strategies introduced in Chapter 1, "The Good Strategy User":

1. self-management strategies that deal with issues such as time management, use of resources, and acquisition of background skills; and
2. thinking strategies that deal with the structuring and use of information.

This chapter explores both kinds of strategies as they apply to science and engineering problem-solving courses and labs.

MANAGING YOUR PROBLEM-SOLVING ACTIVITIES

In order to manage your problem-solving activities effectively, you should do the following:

- Work on Your Problem-Solving Courses Regularly
- Solve Problems on Your Own
- Do Some *Uncalculated* Solutions
- Choose Problems Wisely
- Set a Time Limit
- Develop Useful Help Resources
- Have the Necessary Background and Skills
- Keep Your Attitudes Positive

Work on Your Problem-Solving Courses Regularly

Schedule regular periods in the week for working on each of your problem-solving courses. This is very important for two reasons:

1. Problem-solving courses are often sequential, and so understanding today's concept often depends on knowing last week's material.
2. At times, you will need help in learning about concepts and their application, and this can't be done at the last minute just before a test.

Solve Problems on Your Own

Many students avoid getting down to solving problems by spending too much time rereading the text and lecture notes or looking at examples of solved problems. Because exams in these courses require that you solve problems on your own, you need to practise doing just that. Therefore, you should try to learn the basics of each concept as quickly as possible, and then get right into trying to solve the relevant problems. This also means concentrating on learning the basics in the lecture (as opposed to just making notes) so that you can minimize the time you have to spend reading over the ideas after class. Once you understanding the basic concepts, re-solve the solved examples in both the text and the lecture, and then start the practice problems.

Do Some *Uncalculated* Solutions

You do *not* have to solve every practice problem completely. In an uncalculated solution, you only set up the solution, but you do *not* actually carry out the arithmetic or algebraic calculations to get a final answer. Because the complete solution to many problems requires considerable calculation, doing this with every second or third problem you tackle can save you considerable study time. However, you should use this strategy only if you have first successfully and completely solved a few problems with the new concept and if your arithmetic or algebraic skills do *not* need improvement.

Choose Problems Wisely

You do *not* have to solve all the practice problems. Many students waste a considerable amount of time and energy slavishly trying to solve every practice problem available. Some students do this because they believe that they will learn how to solve each and every possible problem, while others believe that "more is always better." Remember that your goal in doing practice problems is to learn how to apply a given concept to solve a variety of relevant problems. Usually, there are only a few significantly different kinds of difficult problems associated with a given concept. (See "Range of Problems Strategy" on page 127.) Therefore, choose a few easy problems first to see if you can apply the concept confidently. Then look for appropriate problems that are difficult in a significantly different way, and do only as many of those as you need to feel fairly confident. For example, most math, chemistry, and physics texts have at least 50 practice problems associated with a single concept, usually in increasing order of difficulty. By choosing wisely, you might have to do only fifteen to twenty of those 50 problems to gain the confidence needed to apply the concept correctly to any possible exam question.

Set a Time Limit

Many students easily get hooked when trying to solve a problem and spend an hour or two making little progress. Unfortunately, if you do run across a few problems like this, you can expend a lot of study time and have very little, other than frustration, to show for it. This getting-hooked pattern is certainly a major factor in the failure of many science and engineering students. So, plan to attempt at least four problems in one hour. Use a timer if necessary, and after the first fifteen minutes, go on to the next problem even if you are stuck on the first one. What do you do about the problems you cannot solve? The next strategy suggests some ways to get "unstuck."

Develop Useful Help Resources

When stuck on a problem, most students typically consult their lecture notes and text, but often these resources do not help. However, there are other help resources such as the instructor, tutorial assistant, help centre, tutors, other students (small groups of two to four students working on problems together), different texts, and solution books (e.g., Schaum's Outline Series, a resource containing many worked examples of problems for courses in math, physics, economics, and other problem-based disciplines). The World Wide Web also has sites that display solved problems in a variety of courses. Good Strategy Users often use a greater range of help resources than less successful students do. However, to use resources effectively, you need to identify your specific difficulties as concisely as you can and, of course, you actually have to go for help.

Have the Necessary Background and Skills

Because problem-solving courses such as statistics and physics are required courses for certain programs or degrees, there is a great temptation to attempt these courses without having the adequate background knowledge and skills. This can make a difficult course just about impossible. To avoid this trap, make an early investigation into any problem-solving courses you need to take. Talk to the instructor, get a course outline or old exam, and see what kind of background is really necessary. If your background is weak, there are a variety of ways you can remedy that. Many institutions have specialized learning centres that offer diagnostic testing and self-paced instruction. Correspondence high-school courses are also available in a variety of subjects. If your weaknesses are not very serious, you could strengthen your knowledge and skills by working through an appropriate text on your own.

Keep Your Attitudes Positive

It is all too common to hear statements from unsuccessful students such as: "I hate calculus. There are so many formulas to memorize in physics. You have to be a nerd to really get that stuff." Negative attitudes such as these can be very damaging to your effectiveness as a learner in a problem-solving course. Monitor what you are saying to yourself or to others about the problem-solving courses you are taking. If negative attitudes and beliefs are creeping in, try replacing them with more positive but realistic self-talk such as: "If I work on understanding this stuff, I can get it. There's got to be a fairly simple idea underneath all this. I must be missing something because I know it's not meant to be that difficult." You might try asking a few successful students how they view the course and evaluate how their comments compare to your own. Try to foster a positive attitude to the courses you take.

THREE KEY THINKING STRATEGIES

Educational research indicates that there are very real differences in the way in which successful and unsuccessful students approach problem solving in science and engineering. As discussed in Chapter 5, unsuccessful students have been found to favour an unstructured, formula-memorizing approach, while successful students opt for an information-structuring or conceptual approach. In other words, unsuccessful students memorize many specific formulas and solutions, and then try to match them to the problem at hand. However, Good Strategy Users learn how to apply a few key formulas and a small amount of important conceptual information to many different situations. Fortunately, research also shows that students can become more successful problem-solvers by learning to use this conceptual approach.

The conceptual approach to science problem solving involves three separate but interconnected learning goals as shown below. The specific strategy recommended for each of these three goals is identified in brackets after the activity:

GOAL #1   Learning and understanding the small amount of information essential to each concept you learn. *(Concept Summary)*

GOAL #2   Learning how to apply this small amount of conceptual information to solve actual problems. *(Decision Steps)*

GOAL #3   Learning to anticipate and prepare for the more difficult problems that often appear on exams. *(Range of Problems)*

These three specific strategies, which will be discussed in greater detail shortly, are intended to help you develop a more conceptual approach to problem-solving courses and to discourage simple formula memorizing. They recommend that you summarize and record key information for every concept that you are taught. At first, this act of recording information may seem awkward; however, most students report that this strategic approach produces improved results.

You may also find it difficult to organize your learning consciously around concepts, especially if you tended to be a formula-memorizer in the past. So how do you identify a concept? Concepts are the main topics in the course, so you can find them in the course outline or in the table of contents of your textbook. Typically, concepts involve a few very powerful general ideas that are usually expressed as key formulas. The mole in chemistry, the limit of a function in mathematics, the t-test in statistics, and Newton's second law in physics would all be examples of concepts. However, determining a single concept in a lecture or chapter can be a little tricky at first, so it is better to group smaller concepts into one larger chunk of information for convenience. For example, the concepts of acid, base, and pH can be grouped together as one concept rather than as three separate ones.

When you solve problems using the conceptual approach, you must learn to apply correctly *only* the key and relevant conceptual formulas to the specific situation represented in the problem. For example, many quite complex physics problems involving masses and pulleys can be solved by repeated and careful application of the concept of Newton's second law and the one key formula that accompanies it. Unfortunately, many formula-memorizing students try to learn a specific and different formula for each of these problems rather than learning how to apply the one key formula.

Now, let's take a closer look at the following three key thinking strategies discussed earlier:

- Concept Summary Strategy
- Decision Steps Strategy
- Range of Problems Strategy

Concept Summary Strategy

As in other types of courses, students in problem-solving courses need to use a framework or checklist to select and organize the crucial information. The concept summary is one such framework that you can use (see Figure 8.1). For each concept you encounter, keep track of most or all of the following five items and make a brief written summary for each concept.

- Allowable Key Formula(s)
- Definitions
- Additional Important Information
- Simple Examples or Explanations
- List of Relevant Knowns and Unknowns

Allowable Key Formula(s)
Usually, a specific concept consists of one or a few more key formulas that you are allowed to use. All other related formulas are special cases that can be derived easily from these first principles, so these other formulas should not be learned. If you have trouble identifying which formulas are the key ones, ask the instructor or look on the summary page of the text.

Definitions
To apply a key formula correctly, you need to know what each term means. Therefore, you need to define every new term in the formulas, including units and symbols.

Additional Important Information
This is information needed to apply the formulas correctly: sign conventions, special characteristics of terms, reference values, the meaning of zero values, and sit-

uations in which the key formulas do not work. For example, the slope of a line is positive if the line slopes upward, negative if the line slopes downward, and zero if the line is flat.

Simple Examples or Explanations

Providing simple examples or explanations in your own words, diagrams, or analogies is a good test of understanding. Expressing the basics of a concept in different ways forces you to think more deeply about the concept. Often, just thinking about a simple example or analogy and sketching a diagram of the concept at work can be very helpful in this regard.

List of Relevant Knowns and Unknowns

When faced with a variety of problems to solve, many students find it difficult to know which concept applies to which problem. To avoid this difficulty, list the crucial knowns and unknowns (and their common synonyms) that need to be presented in a problem in order to signal to you that this particular concept should be applied. For example, problems in Newton's second law and problems in kinematics may both ask for or give the acceleration of an object. However, problems in Newton's second law also include mass and force, while those in kinematics involve velocities and time.

FIGURE 8.1   AN EXAMPLE OF A CONCEPT SUMMARY

<u>Concept</u>: Straight-line Kinematics: Constant Acceleration

<u>Allowable Key Formulas</u>:

1. $\vec{V}_f = \vec{V}_i + \vec{a}\,(\Delta t)$ 2. $\vec{X}_f = \vec{X}_i + \vec{V}_i\,(\Delta t) + \frac{1}{2}\vec{a}\,(\Delta t)^2$

3. $\vec{V}_f^{\,2} = \vec{V}_i^{\,2} + 2\vec{a}\,(\Delta \vec{X})$

<u>Definitions</u>:

$\vec{V}_i$ and $\vec{V}_f$ are initial and final velocities of object in m/s

$\vec{a}$ is acceleration of object in m/s²

$\vec{X}_i$ and $\vec{X}_f$ are initial and final positions of object in m

Δt is time taken for object to move from $\vec{X}_i$ to $\vec{X}_f$ in s

(continued)

(continued)

<u>Additional Important Information</u>:

1. $\vec{x}, \vec{v}, \vec{a}$ are <u>vector</u> quantities. $\therefore$ choose a + direction in a problem and be consistent.

2. $g = 9.8 \ ^{m}/s^2$ downward.

3. When $\vec{a} = 0$ object moves with constant velocity.

4. These formulas <u>only</u> work for one value of constant acceleration.

<u>Explanation</u>:

These formulas relate <u>2</u> points on path of object undergoing constant acceleration

<u>List of Relevant Knowns and Unknowns</u>:

Use these formulas with problems (or parts of) that involve:

1. "acceleration" or "speeding up," "slowing down," "braking," "coming to rest"

2. "velocities" or "speeds"—assuming direction is known

3. "positions," "displacements," or distances (assumed direction)

4. "time" taken for object to move between 2 points

Decision Steps Strategy

Good problem solving involves making accurate decisions about which concepts apply to specific situations. It is easy to follow the instructor's accurate decisions about how to apply a specific concept to a problem, but when you are faced with a new problem to solve on your own, it is often difficult to know where to start—that is, what decision is first? If you are like many students, you may try to handle this situation by either plugging numbers into formulas blindly or trying to memorize every solution. Neither of these approaches works very well. A better approach is to keep track of the decision steps you need to follow in order to solve problems logically from first principles (i.e., concept summary).

Decision steps focus on the key decisions that lead to the correct application of a concept instead of focussing on the computations that are actually the result of applying good decision steps. Frequently, instructors will state in lectures the decision steps that they are following, but they do not usually write them down. As a result, many students focus on the mathematical equations and computations that are written down and not on the decision steps that generated them. Therefore, try at some point to record these decision steps in words and not in mathematical notation. After revising your decision steps once or twice, you may want to record them more neatly beside one or two solved examples (as shown in Figures 8.2, 8.3, and 8.4).

Therefore, the decision steps strategy involves the following:

- Record Decision Steps in Your Own Words
- Use and Revise Your Decision Steps

Record Decision Steps in Your Own Words

The steps of correctly solved examples should be carefully analyzed by answering one or more of these questions for each step:

- What was done in this step?
- How was it done (i.e., which formula or guideline was used)?
- Why was it done?

Good decision steps can clarify basic problem-solving tasks for specific concepts by identifying knowns and unknowns and applying formulas as needed. To be most useful, decision steps should be brief and focus on steps you find tricky.

Use and Revise Your Decision Steps

After you have a few decision steps based on the analysis of a solved example, try to "test run" these steps on a similar problem. Usually, your initial decision steps are imperfect and incomplete, so revision is needed.

FIGURE 8.2 DECISION STEPS APPLIED TO A SOLVED PHYSICS PROBLEM

Problem

A police car begins accelerating from rest at 2.0 m/s^2 in pursuit of a pair of bank robbers who are travelling in a getaway car at a constant velocity of 20 m/s. If the police were originally 100 m behind when they started, when and where will they catch the bank robbers?

Steps	Solution

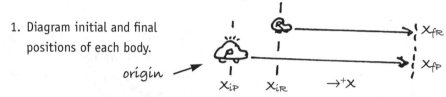

1. Diagram initial and final positions of each body.

   origin →

   X_{iP} X_{iR} →^+X

2. Choose +X direction and origin.

3. Make a table identifying initial and final values for each body. Note:
   • Watch signs!
   • X_i's depend on origin.

   <u>Police</u>

   $V_i = 0$

   $a = {}^+2\,m/s^2$

   $X_{iP} = 0$

   $X_{fP} = ?$ ← *same*

   $\Delta t = ?$ ← "

   <u>Robbers</u>

   $V_{iR} = V_{fR} = {}^+20\,m/s$

   $a = 0$

   $X_{iR} = {}^+100\,m$

   → $X_{fR} = ?$

   → $\Delta t = ?$

4. Apply this formula to each body:
   $X_f = X_i + V_i(\Delta t) + \tfrac{1}{2}a(\Delta t)^2$
   (i.e., produce 2 equations)

   $X_{fP} = 0 + 0 + \tfrac{1}{2}(2)(\Delta t)^2 = (\Delta t)^2$

   $X_{fR} = 100 + 20\,(\Delta t)$

5. Relate these 2 equations. (usually they are equal)

   $\therefore (\Delta t)^2 = 100 + 20\,(\Delta t)$

   → $\Delta t = 24.1s$ (by quadratic)

6. Solve and check answers to see if X_f's are equal. (note: report answer noting your origin)

   $\therefore X_{fP} = 581m$

   $\S X_{fR} = 582m$ ⟩ ok

   from where police started

FIGURE 8.3   DECISION STEPS FOR ACID-BASE PROBLEMS IN CHEMISTRY[6]

Problem

Find the pH of a solution prepared by adding 300mL of 0.100 M acetic acid and 200 mL of 0.100 M NaOH. (K_a of acetic acid is 1.85×10^{-5})

Steps	Solution

1. Identify each species in problem.
   4 possibilities:
   a) strong acid or base → know these!
   b) weak acid or base → not strong!
   c) conjugate acid or base
   d) spectator salt

- acetic acid (HAc) → <u>weak</u> acid
- NaOH → <u>strong</u> base

∴ <u>there is acid-base reaction</u>
   $HAc = (0.300l)(0.100M)$

   $= 0.030$ moles

2. Is there an acid-base reaction?
   (except weak and its conjugate)
   If No → go to step 3
   If Yes:
   a) Write acid/base reaction (with no back reaction!)
   b) Do stoichiometry on this reaction to find what's left.

& $OH^- = 0.020$ moles

∴ $HAc + OH^- \rightarrow Ac^- + H_2O$

I: 0.030   0.020 $\emptyset$

R: $\underline{0.020}$ $\underline{0.020}$ $+0.020$
F: 0.010 $\emptyset$ 0.020

∴ weak & conjugate left
   is buffer (possibility a)

   [I can use moles]

3. Identify what's left.
   4 possibilities:
   a) If weak & conjugate left → use buffer equation (moles or concentration).
   b) If conjugate only left →
      • find its concentration
      • set up equil. equation for conj. $+ H_2O \rightleftharpoons$ weak $+ OH^-$ or H_3O^+
      • $K_w = K_a K_b$
   c) If strong only → find pH by simply finding OH^- or H_3O^+ concentration of strong.
   d) If strong only → find other ion concentration use common ion.

∴ $HAc + H_2O \rightleftharpoons Ac^- + H_3O^+$

E: 0.010   0.020   x

Set up Ka:

$\rightarrow 1.85 \times 10^{-5} = \dfrac{(0.020)(x)}{0.010}$

$\rightarrow x = 9.25 \times 10^{-6} M$

∴ pH $= 5.03$

---

[6] Based on steps by Dr. Colin Baird.

FIGURE 8.4   DECISION STEPS FOR ARC LENGTH IN CALCULUS[7]

1. Sketch graph of the function.
2. Decide whether to do it as a function of x or function of y. (Note: Sometimes problem can be done either way, but <u>be clear</u> about whether to integrate over x interval or y interval.)
3. Recall general formula for arc length.

$$s = \int_a^b \sqrt{1 + (^{dy}/_{dx})^2}\, dx \ \text{ or } \ s = \int_c^d \sqrt{1 + (^{dx}/_{dy})^2}\, dy$$

4. Identify limits of integration for problem.
5. Find first derivative of function given in the problem.
6. Substitute into arc length formula.
7. Check to see if problem gives any specific instructions about evaluating the integral. *Some possibilities:*
   - set up integral but don't evaluate
   - use a numerical method
   - use integration techniques

Problem: Find the arc length of the graph of $y = 5 - (\frac{4}{3})x^{(3/2)}$ from x = 0 to x = 4

Solution:

$$y = f(x) = 5 - \frac{4}{3}x^{3/2}$$

$$\therefore \text{ Integrate over } x$$

$$\rightarrow a = 0; \ b = 4$$

$$\text{and } \frac{dy}{dx} = f'(x) = -\frac{4}{3}\left(\frac{3}{2}\right)x^{1/2} = -2x^{1/2}$$

$$\text{Now: } s = \int_0^4 \sqrt{1 + (-2x^{1/2})^2}\, dx = \int_0^4 \sqrt{1 + 4x}\, dx$$

$$\text{Integrate and get: } s = \frac{1}{6}(1 + 4x)^{3/2}\Big|_0^4$$

$$\rightarrow s = \frac{1}{6}[17^{3/2} - 1] \cong 11.5$$

(graph annotations: +y, (0, 5), $y = 5 - \frac{4}{3}x^{3/2}$, +x, (4, $-17/3$))

---

[7] The decision steps that are associated with the concept of arc length have been written out separately and then applied to this problem. This example was provided by Maaike Froelich.

Range of Problems Strategy

The practice problems in a textbook associated with a specific concept usually start with quite easy problems and then increase in difficulty. Unfortunately, it is often the more difficult problems that show up on the test. Usually, there are only a few significantly different types of difficult problems associated with a given concept. The majority of practice problems are just minor variations of one of these types. This strategy of identifying the range of problems helps you to identify some of the common types of difficult problems associated with a specific concept. The intention in doing this is to change your perspective from that of a passive receiver who hopes for easy problems but often receives difficult ones to that of a strategist who can effectively anticipate and solve the full range of problems from the easiest to the most difficult. For a Good Strategy User, the range of problems strategy involves the following:

- Know the Common Kinds of Difficult Problems
- Anticipate the Different Kinds of Difficult Problems
- List the Range of Problems from Easy to Difficult

Know the Common Kinds of Difficult Problems

Here are most of the common kinds of difficult problems (feel free to add others):

- **Hidden knowns:** Needed information is hidden in a phrase or diagram (e.g., "at rest" means v=0).
- **Multipart — same concept:** A problem may comprise two or more subproblems, each involving the use of the same concept. This type of problem can be solved only by identifying the given information in the light of these subproblems.
- **Multipart — different concepts:** Same idea as above, except now the subproblems involve the use of different concepts.
- **Multipart — simultaneous equations:** Same idea as above, except no one subproblem can be solved fully by itself. You may have two unknowns and two equations or three unknowns and three equations, and you will have to solve them simultaneously, (e.g., through substitution, comparison, addition and subtraction, or matrices, etc.).
- **Work backward:** Some problems look difficult because to solve them you have to work in reverse order from problems that you have previously solved.
- **Letters only:** When known quantities are expressed in letters, problems can look difficult, but if you follow the decision steps, these are not usually so difficult.

- **"Dummy" variables:** Sometimes a quantity that you feel should be a known is not specified because it is not really needed—that is, it cancels out (e.g., mass in work-energy problems, temperature in gas-law problems).
- **Red herrings (extra information):** A problem may give you more information than you need. This can be unnerving if you expect to use all the given information.

Anticipate the Different Kinds of Difficult Problems

As you attempt the practice problems associated with a specific concept, anticipate that different kinds of difficult problems should be arising, and be ready to solve them. Typically, then, the first few problems associated with a new concept will be fairly straightforward applications of the key formula(s). As you progress through the problems, though, you will start to see some that need to be worked backward, others with hidden knowns, two- and three-part problems, and so on.

List the Range of Problems from Easy to Difficult

After you have finished studying a specific concept, make a list of the range of problem types from easy to difficult that you encountered as well as any other difficult types that are likely and "testable." Include a brief reference to a specific example for each type of difficult problem you identify. (See Figure 8.5.)

SUCCESS IN THE LAB

Many science and engineering courses require a few hours working in the lab each week and often more hours at home completing the lab report. This lab component can be worth a significant portion of the final grade, and it focusses on hands-on learning that is quite different from the conceptual learning that occurs in lectures. To handle this practical learning situation effectively, you need to apply the following relevant learning strategies:

- Find Connections between the Labs and the Course Material
- Determine How Much Each Lab Report Is Worth
- Prepare Effectively for Each Lab
- Use Your Lab Time Wisely
- Get Lab Reports Done Quickly

FIGURE 8.5 AN EXAMPLE OF A RANGE OF PROBLEMS

> (STRAIGHT-LINE KINEMATICS—CONST. ACCEL)
>
> I.   1-Body problems:
>   a. 1 part (i.e. 1 pair of initial & final pts.)
>   1. "Simple"-no change in direction
>   e.g. cyclist accelerates.
>   2. "Change direction"-esp up/down
>   e.g. ball goes up & down.
>
>   b. 2 or more parts (i.e. more than 1 pair of initial
>   and final pts.).
>   1. one acceleration: pts A→B, B→C, etc...
>   e.g. rock falls $\frac{1}{2}$ height of cliff in last second...
>   how high is cliff?
>   2. two or more accelerations: e.g. train speeds up,
>   slows down, constant velocity, comes to stop.
>
>   c. Find Average Velocity (v_{arg}): for problems above
>
>
> II. 2-Body problems:
>   a. Simultaneous equations required:
>   1. Initial x's are different, e.g. police & robbers
>   2. Initial t's are different, e.g. coconuts off cliff.

Explanation

The student here has classified all the problems she has seen that are associated with this concept into "subtypes" that identify important differences in the structure and difficulty of the problems. Note that many subtypes are specific examples of the ways to make problems difficult. The student has also included key words about specific examples that typify that subtype, e.g., cyclist problems.

Find Connections between the Labs and the Course Material

The lab component gives students a very different and practical way of experiencing the concepts and ideas taught in lectures. Sometimes the connection between lab and lecture is obvious, but often students mistakenly feel that the two are almost totally separate entities. Whenever you are working on a lab, give some thought to the connections between it and the relevant course material. For example, you will often be asked to show that a particular theory or law can adequately explain the behaviour of a specific system you measure in the lab. Make sure you know the theory or law before going to the lab, and keep it in mind as you work on the lab. By using this strategy, you take advantage of the memory principle of association, which can help your learning both in the lab and in the lecture.

Determine How Much Each Lab Report Is Worth

Many students make the mistake of working far too many hours trying to write the perfect lab report. It is essential that you spend only as much time on each lab as it is worth. Usually, the lab component is worth from 15 to 40 percent of your overall final grade, so that with five to ten lab reports due, the value of a single lab report varies from about 2 to 8 percent of your final grade. Therefore, you should plan to spend no more than two to eight hours on the report. Remember that term tests and quizzes are often worth much more than lab reports and thus merit more of your study time.

Prepare Effectively for Each Lab

Read over the description of each lab in the lab manual *shortly before* you go to the actual lab session. Often, these descriptions appear to be quite complex initially, but you can simplify your preparation if you look for the following common features of most lab descriptions and find the important details that usually accompany them (you can consider this to be the lab framework):

- **Introduction:** Purpose of the lab and introduction of the relevant concepts or theories.
- **Method:** Equipment and procedure you will use to achieve purpose (also note any special safety precautions).

- **Results:** The observations, data, diagrams, graphs, or products that you will produce in the lab. Do you need to make any data tables, diagrams, or sample calculations before coming to the lab?
- **Conclusion:** The analysis and presentation of your lab results in the lab report.

Use Your Lab Time Wisely

There are always a few students who manage to work through the lab more quickly and effectively than the rest of the class. Listed below are some of the strategies they use to get the most out of their lab time. Use this list to check both which of these you are currently using and which ones you should be using.

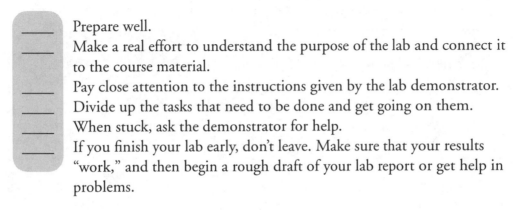

_____ Prepare well.

_____ Make a real effort to understand the purpose of the lab and connect it to the course material.

_____ Pay close attention to the instructions given by the lab demonstrator.

_____ Divide up the tasks that need to be done and get going on them.

_____ When stuck, ask the demonstrator for help.

_____ If you finish your lab early, don't leave. Make sure that your results "work," and then begin a rough draft of your lab report or get help in problems.

Get Lab Reports Done Quickly

If you have been using a number of the lab strategies described above, the actual writing of the report should not be very difficult or time-consuming. However, there are still some things you can do at this stage.

First, make sure you know what the lab instructor expects to see in a good lab report. Usually you will be given instructions on how to write the lab report, but, if possible, it is better to see an actual model lab report. Often the lab instructor will make a model report available.

Second, use a computer or a programmable calculator to save time whenever possible. This includes using a spreadsheet program to do repetitive calculations and produce any resulting graphs quickly. If you don't know how to use a spreadsheet program, learn! Mastering the basic operations of such a program does not take long and will save you a lot of calculation and graphing time. Also, use a word processor to write the report. You might even consider using a graphics program for specialized diagrams.

Third, avoid the temptation to make the lab report perfect. If you have adequately covered each of the main features expected in a good report, then stop working.

THE DAY-BY-DAY PROBLEM-SOLVER

Box 8.1 demonstrates how a Good Strategy User enrolled in a problem-solving course would use many of the strategies described in this chapter on a day-to-day basis. You can use this as a summary and checklist of the strategies in this chapter.

BOX 8.1 PROBLEM-SOLVING CHECKLIST

Just before Lecture

☑ Maintain a positive attitude by remembering that a concept actually has very little information (but that information must be learned well).

During Lecture

☑ Go into class intending to learn as much as possible in the lecture.
☑ Watch for components of the concept summary.
☑ Focus on decision steps whenever an example is solved.

After Lecture (for fifteen to thirty minutes)

☑ Fill in the review column of your lecture notes.
☑ Again track components of the concept summary (especially key formulas).
☑ Carefully analyze any solved examples to identify decision steps.
☑ If in doubt, refer to text.

(continued)

(continued)

During That Same Week

☑ Make the concept summary.

☑ Learn components of this concept summary well.

☑ Write initial decision steps beside or near a solved example.

☑ Re-solve other lecture examples on your own by following these decision steps.

☑ Start solving practice problems by choosing a few easy, then some medium and some difficult ones.

☑ Always use your decision steps to solve practice problems.

☑ Revise your decision steps as you work through a variety of problems.

☑ Anticipate common kinds of difficult problems.

☑ Limit the time you spend on each problem you attempt.

☑ Maintain a positive attitude — problems are not meant to be *that* difficult.

☑ If stuck, get help promptly.

For Labs

☑ Use preparation and in-lab strategies.

☑ Spend only a reasonable time on the lab report.

Before Exams

☑ List the range of problems for each concept to be tested.

☑ Practise solving problems out of context by using old tests or sheets of review problems. You can also put individual problems on slips of paper, mix them in a jar, and then select a problem to be solved. The same effect can be achieved by typing problems into a computer and then randomly selecting ones to be solved.

STRATEGIES CAN MAKE THE DIFFERENCE

PROBLEM SOLVING, either at a theoretical level or in a laboratory setting, has long been at the core of teaching and learning in science and engineering courses, especially in subjects such as math, physics, and chemistry. This chapter has taken a careful look at ways in which you can optimize your success in such problem-based courses. Continuing the theme of the student as the Good Strategy User, the chapter began by listing self-management strategies that stress the importance of timely and constant reinforcement of ideas. The questions that you choose to solve, your time management, and your use of resources are as important as are your thinking strategies that lead to your eventually solving the problems.

Three specific thinking strategies were described through examples: the concept summary strategy, the decision steps strategy, and the range of problems strategy. Applied regularly, these three strategies lead to sound understanding and retention of science concepts and processes.

In addition to theoretical problem solving, many science and engineering courses include a laboratory component. This chapter has stressed how important it is for you to be well prepared and to use your time wisely in the lab. If you can leave each lab with most, if not all, of the necessary work completed, you will have made strategic use of your time and resources. The next chapter, "Preparing for Exams," focusses on what you can do to prepare effectively for examinations.

CHAPTER 9

Preparing for Exams

LEARNING OBJECTIVES

The purpose of this chapter is for you to:

→ Reflect on the way you prepare for exams now.
→ Learn about the three important steps in exam preparation and the strategies that accompany these steps.
→ Learn about common exam-review techniques that do not work well.
→ Consider how best to prepare for final exams.

I N MOST COURSES, examinations are a major factor in your overall grade, and so how you go about preparing for them will have a considerable impact on your success as a student. We will assume that you attended all of your classes, that you have an excellent set of class notes from which to study, and that you completed your text readings and other assignments regularly. Preparation for exams is easier if you are reviewing material that you have spent time consolidating each week. At the same time, however, effective review just before the exam will allow you to gain a wider perspective of the course content than is possible from your week-to-week work.

This chapter stresses the importance of knowing what to expect on the exam *before* your final review. The main message of this chapter, though, is that your review should involve two distinctly different processes: inputting and outputting information. Many students focus only on inputting information—by reading over notes, texts, and other relevant materials. The Good Strategy User, however, also stresses output through self-testing and recalling information from long-term memory. If these are an integral part of your review process, writing the exam itself is less of a challenge.

STUDENT COMMENTS ON EXAMS

On the following list of statements by students about exams, check those that apply to you. In each case, is your answer what you think would reflect the Good Strategy User? Feel free to add observations of your own about exams.

_____ 1. I have to be in the right mood to get down to studying for exams.
_____ 2. I know exactly what each of my tests is worth.
_____ 3. I don't really know how much time I should spend studying for exams.
_____ 4. If I try to plan an exam study schedule, it ends up taking a lot of potential study time.
_____ 5. It is difficult to limit the amount of study time I spend preparing for exams.
_____ 6. I tend to skip the last class before exams so that I can study.
_____ 7. Reading the text is the best preparation for any test.
_____ 8. Multiple-choice exams are tricky.

____ 9. You don't need to know as much to answer multiple-choice exams.
____ 10. I always do better on essay questions.
____ 11. I try to begin writing as soon as possible in an exam.
____ 12. Exams give me a chance to really understand the course.
____ 13. I like to make study notes and to put all the important information together.
____ 14. I learn much better if I work in a study group.

15. _____

16. _____

17. _____

18. _____

WHERE DO YOU START?

Randy loves history and would like to major in it eventually. He spends a lot of time each week reading both the texts and additional readings. He makes summary notes as he reads and is confident of having a good grasp of the major topics for this test.

Linda has been swamped this last month with two major assignments. Last week she was sick for three days and missed several classes, including history. She likes the subject but hasn't put in a lot of time and is worried about this test.

These two students have to write a history test in three days, but from the brief case studies, you can see that each will be starting the review process from very different positions. Randy has already covered a lot more of the basic information and will be able to spend time reviewing material that he has studied before, whereas Linda will probably have to do a lot of reading for the first time.

Any discussion of the review process must acknowledge the basic fact that not all students are equally prepared. Ideally, review should be just that—a viewing again of information already studied. However, it is not uncommon to find students, like Linda, for whom "review" actually means studying new information. In those cases, it becomes a real challenge.

Goals for the review process will be the same for all students, regardless of how well you are prepared to this point. They are:

☑ To understand key concepts and important details.
☑ To have good memory of the course content and the ability to recall relevant information readily.
☑ To know the requirements of typical test questions and be able to apply information in an appropriate manner.

IMPORTANT STEPS IN EXAM PREPARATION

In most courses, exams account for a large percentage of your overall mark. Therefore, it is important that you have a set of strategies you can use in the week or so before the exam that will make your preparation as effective as possible. This section presents a three-step process that includes a number of useful strategies you can use for exam preparation (see Figure 9.1). The three steps are:

• Step 1: Know What to Expect on the Exam
• Step 2: Plan Your Review Activities
• Step 3: Make the Review an Active Learning Process

FIGURE 9.1 THREE STEPS IN EXAM PREPARATION

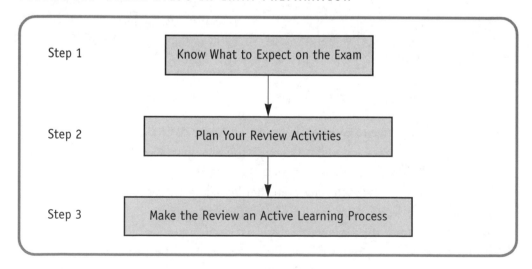

Step 1: Know What to Expect on the Exam

Good Strategy Users find out as much as possible about a test, and so for those of you who do pick up as many cues as possible, some of the following questions may seem like common sense. However, not all students do this, and this is reflected in their marks. The amount of time you can reasonably devote to review depends on your other commitments. Apply the following questions to your next test:

- When, where, and how long is the test?
- What format will be used?
- What topics will be covered? Are they from lectures, readings, labs, seminars, etc.?
- What special interests of the instructor might influence the topics, format, etc.?
- Are any old exams or practice questions available?
- What resources are available for help during the review process—instructors, teaching assistants, other students, help centre, the Internet?
- What percentage of the final grade is this test worth?
- What grade can you realistically aim for?

Step 2: Plan Your Review Activities

Whether you are beginning from a good base or not, it is very important to plan your review. Someone who already has a sound knowledge base can spend much more time practising applying that information to sample questions, whereas a student who has a lot of basic make-up work to do will need to fill in missing information. Here are some strategies to help you plan your review:

- **Set targets.** Choose your own targets on what is to be completed by what date. Setting up a plan seems to motivate many students by giving them measurable goals to aim for.
- **Decide where to work.** Avoid settings with obvious distractions or interruptions from friends.
- **Identify topics that need special attention because you find them most difficult.** This task in itself is difficult for some students, and they have to consider seriously which topics these are. You may need to get help during the review process if you are unclear on important concepts.
- **Plan the order in which you will go through the content.** This may be tied to the cues that you picked up from the instructor. It is not uncommon

for the heaviest weight to be given to the topics most recently completed. Therefore, these should get special attention.

- **Aim to know the most important topics very well.** If you do not have time to study everything, then it is better to focus on the topics that you want to know really well rather than aim to cover everything inadequately. If possible, target sections that you think will pay off most.
- **Plan ways to evaluate the quality of your review.** How will you test yourself and evaluate your progress? If old exams are available, make sure that you have copies. If there are study-guide questions, plan when you will use them.
- **Make arrangements with other students to study together.** Group study can be effective if there is a clear agenda for such meetings. Plan to do this well ahead of the test.

Step 3: Make the Review an Active Learning Process

For many students, review means passively "just reading the material over." While this technique is fairly easy to do, it rarely works well. Review needs to be an active process that involves you in two important activities:

- Information Gathering
- Information Using

Although your information-gathering phase of the review usually comes first, it may be necessary to switch back and forth a few times between these two activities as your review proceeds.

Information Gathering

Information gathering involves refamiliarizing yourself with all the sources of information for the course. Class notes are often of prime importance because instructors highlight primary concepts in lectures. Other important information will be in the text, lab notes, essays, old exams, and handouts. In fact, test questions can be drawn from any part of the course. This is why the issue of figuring out the role of the lecture and text discussed in Chapter 6, "Learning from Lectures," and Chapter 7, "Learning from Textbooks," is so important. Ideally, by the time you have to review for a test, you will already have summarized course content through highlighting or as summary notes, and will not then have to reread the original sources.

Here are three active learning strategies for effective information gathering:

1. **Pull together one set of headings (themes and subthemes).** Often, one lecture topic will overlap with the text topic, so eliminate duplication of review by deciding which source has more "testable" material and working primarily from that. From other sources, add in material that does not overlap with your main source. A good course outline can be the best guide for identifying headings. If you do not have a useful course outline, you will need to generate this list for yourself.
2. **Learn this set of headings.** These subthemes are all part of the big picture. Their order in the course is not random, so it is important to try to see the logic behind that order. Recite these main headings to fix them firmly into long-term memory. This should be easier if you see how they form a big picture. Remember that instructors often use headings as a first step to creating test questions.
3. **Make sure you have identified, understood, and summarized all the important details that go with each heading.** You can select important details based on the patterns of main ideas as discussed in Chapter 5, "Effective Memory." Key terms are often highlighted as bold or italicized text or in a glossary. Knowing these important details is essential to successful test performance. You may need to get help from the instructor if there is anything that you do not fully understand.

Information Using

Information using is a crucial and all too often forgotten activity. To do well on a test, it is not enough to be organized and to have read through all the information. You also have to be able to apply the information to answer the test questions. To be able to do this well, you need to *rehearse* the type of thought processes that the test will demand—recalling or applying information to typical test-like questions. How do you do this? In order to answer this question, it is important to have some idea of the way in which many instructors design test questions.

One especially useful and influential approach to the design of exam questions was devised by an educational psychologist named Benjamin Bloom. He proposed a model—now called "Bloom's Taxonomy"—to summarize typical learning objectives, one set of which was the cognitive learning objectives. There are six levels of cognitive learning objectives in the model, with each level more demanding than the previous one. This model is commonly used as a guide to writing exam questions since questions can then be devised to test a specific cognitive learning objective. An understanding of this model can help you to rehearse

TABLE 9.1   SIX LEVELS OF COGNITIVE LEARNING OBJECTIVES IN BLOOM'S TAXONOMY

Level	Objective	Example of Type of Test Question
1	Knowledge	Recall definition of key term
2	Comprehension	Identify evidence supporting an argument
3	Application	Apply a concept to a new situation
4	Analysis	Analyze a case study
5	Synthesis	Link ideas to create a new interpretation
6	Evaluation	Criticize an established theory

for exams much more effectively by making you more aware of the variety of questions you may expect. Table 9.1 shows the six levels of cognitive learning objectives in Bloom's Taxonomy.[8]

Note that knowledge recall, often the goal of many students, is only the first and lowest level that instructors use to generate test questions. The other levels require that you use the information you have gathered. Effective review strategies reflect this requirement.

Here are seven active learning strategies for effective information using:

1. **Write or recite all the important details from memory.** When you think you know the information, close your books and test your memory. This strategy is especially important to use in preparing for multiple-choice and short-answer tests that require you to recall the details of information. Although it may not seem so, remembering a lot of new information is not difficult if you can see how each piece of information relates to the big picture.
2. **Generate your own new examples.** This helps you to learn how to apply a concept to a new situation.
3. **Predict and then answer likely test questions.** Because test questions usually ask you to use or apply the important (testable) details that go with a

[8] Bloom, B.S., Englemart, M.D., Furst, E.J., Hill, W.H., & Krathwohl, D.R. (1956). *Taxonomy of educational objectives: The classification of educational goals. Handbook 1: Cognitive domain.* New York: McKay.

particular heading, you can use the headings to create likely test questions, keeping in mind typical patterns of test questions for that course.

4. **Rehearse the whole exam by writing an old exam in test-like conditions.** Don't leave this until the last night before the exam because errors often indicate topics that need more practice.

5. **Spend a lot of time doing varied problems.** If you are being tested through problems, as in science and economics, for example, practise problems that require the application of each of the concepts being tested. It is also very important to review the concepts, close your books, and then do the problems. You need to practise in as realistic a setting as possible where you are drawing only on memory and your own ability to apply the concepts. This is good rehearsal for the exam. Give yourself a reasonable time limit for each question, and if you get stuck, go on to the next question.

6. **Rehearse by writing short essays.** If you are being tested through essays, practise writing these. Too many students make the mistake of only reading for review when the test requires writing. Get used to recalling from memory and writing in a logical, coherent, concise manner.

7. **Make up mnemonics for difficult-to-remember information.** For example many students will remember steps in a complicated process by making a nonsense word that is comprised of the first letter of each step in the process.

COMMON REVIEW TECHNIQUES TO AVOID

Three quite common but ineffective review techniques that you need to watch for and avoid are:

- The "I Know That" Review
- Memorizing without Understanding
- Memorizing Answers

The "I Know That" Review

The "I know that" review[9] is the technique in which the student simply looks at some topic and says "I know that," and then moves to the next topic. The prob-

---

[9] Suggested by Marco Iafrate.

lem here is that *recognizing* information is not the same as *recalling* it and being able to *use* it to answer a test question.

Memorizing without Understanding

Memorizing the definitions of long lists of terms without trying to understand how they fit into the big picture is an ineffective way to memorize course information. Also, Bloom's Taxonomy suggests that to do well on a exam, you need to be able to do more than recall definitions.

Memorizing Answers

Memorizing the answers to questions from the study guide, solutions manual, or an old exam is ineffective because it is unlikely your exam will use these same questions. Exam-like questions (and answers) from these sources can be useful but only if used in a strategic manner (i.e., you try the questions as a self-testing activity).

FINAL EXAMS

Final exams present special demands because often a student is studying for several courses over a limited time period. This involves assessing the total picture and making some major decisions on when and how long to study for each course.

Students often fall into the trap of overstudying for the first exams, only to run out of time and energy for the later ones. Much will depend on how the exams are spaced. Answer the following questions:

1. How many exams do you have and when are they? Mark the dates on the calendar in Table 9.2 and see how they are spaced.
   To assess your exam activities, record your answers to the following questions in Table 9.3.
2. What course content does each exam cover?
3. What is the format for each?
4. What percentage of the final grade is each worth?
5. Rank each of your courses in terms of the amount of study time it requires for review: 1 = a lot   2 = average   3 = little

TABLE 9.2 BLANK MONTHLY TIMETABLE

MARCH						
S	M	T	W	T	F	S

APRIL						
S	M	T	W	T	F	S

MAY						
S	M	T	W	T	F	S

TABLE 9.3 ASSESSMENT OF EXAM ACTIVITIES

Courses	Material Covered	Format	% of Final Grade	Rank

WORRIED ABOUT EXAMS?

Juan is worried about a major exam he has to take tomorrow morning at 8:00 A.M. He sets his alarm to get up at 5:00 so he will have an extra two hours to read one more chapter. Will he be spending his time in the best way?

_____

_____

_____

Sarah has a 15 percent term test in her 9:00 class and would like some more review time. The instructor in her 8:00 class is returning a major exam that he plans to discuss with the class. Sarah decides to skip her 8:00 class to review for the 9:00 test. Has she made the best decision?

_____

_____

_____

Mark is proud of his notes taken in Psychology 020. He plans to spend five hours reviewing them to ensure a high grade. His friend, Les, has just phoned him and wants to review with him. Mark accepts. Should he have done so?

_____

_____

_____

Sophia knows that she has difficulty in exams in recalling significant points. How can her review be organized so that she does this more easily?

_____

_____

_____

ACTIVE, NOT PASSIVE, REVIEW

THIS CHAPTER HAS emphasized the importance of using an active review process in your exam preparation as opposed to the passive "just read it over" approach favoured by many students. This active review process begins with an assessment of your current level of preparation of the relevant course material: are you up to date, or is there some new information that needs to be covered? Once you are up to date with your course material, the real work of exam preparation can start. Three important steps are involved: the first step is one of gathering as much information about the exam as you can; in the second step, you plan your review by giving some consideration to issues such as how long you need to review, what order of topics will you follow, and how much study time each topic requires; and the third step gives you a number of active strategies you can use to learn the required course material effectively. These active strategies focus on two crucial aspects of successful exam preparation: gathering and using information. It is this two-way process that is the key to effective review.

This chapter, Chapter 5 on effective memory, and Chapters 6 and 7 on learning from lectures and textbooks have presented a variety of thinking strategies for the acquisition and retention of new knowledge. In Part 4, the final focus of *Learning for Success* is the major applications of knowledge: "Writing Exams," "Writing Essays," and "Presenting Seminars." It is by producing excellent work that the Good Strategy User demonstrates the benefits of a quality approach to learning. First, let's examine how to write successful exams.

PART 4

Effective Application of Knowledge

CHAPTER 10

Writing Exams

LEARNING OBJECTIVES

The purpose of this chapter is for you to:

- → Learn strategies for multiple-choice exams.
- → Learn strategies for essay exams.
- → Learn strategies for short-answer exams.
- → Learn strategies for problem-solving exams.
- → Learn strategies for case-study exams.
- → Learn how to manage exam anxiety.

EXAMS ARE THE traditional method for evaluating student performance and progress and are a fact of life for most students. Not all students dislike exams; in fact, some report that upcoming exams produce a sense of excitement and are looked upon as a personal challenge. These students enjoy the feeling of being prepared and well informed about course material, and they also often plan to enjoy a well-earned treat after the exam is over.

Other students experience very different reactions to exams, such as panic and self-doubt. Of course, such negative feelings and thoughts can be justified if a student is unprepared for an exam. However, there are students who experience exam anxiety even when well prepared because they see exams as a threat rather than a personal challenge.

Success in exam writing is largely the result of applying three sets of strategies effectively—as well as adding in a touch of luck! The three sets of strategies have to do first with being well prepared to write the exam, second with applying excellent exam-writing strategies, and third with managing exam anxiety. Chapter 9 dealt with preparing for exams, while this chapter looks first at exam-writing strategies for some common exam formats and then at strategies for coping with exam anxiety.

There are a number of common formats for exams: multiple-choice, essay, short-answer, problem-solving, case-study, true/false, matching-pairs, and fill-in-the-blanks. Each type presents unique demands for the student, who must devise matching strategies. In this chapter, we will examine the five most commonly used formats:

- Multiple-Choice Exams
- Essay Exams
- Short-Answer Exams
- Problem-Solving Exams
- Case-Study Exams

MULTIPLE-CHOICE EXAMS

Multiple-choice exams produce a variety of responses in students. Some claim that they prefer them to essay exams because the questions stimulate considerable recall, and just knowing that the correct answer is on the paper can reduce anxiety. Other students fear multiple-choice exams because they see them as tricky and out to catch them; it is often impossible to choose between at least two seemingly right answers. It is not uncommon for a student to say, "I really knew my stuff, but I had such a hard time with those answers. The mark that I got does not reflect what I knew." Once a student begins to think negatively about multiple-choice exams, that anxiety can escalate, making future exams even more difficult ordeals.

In our work with students, we do a lot of error analysis with multiple-choice exams. This involves working closely with students, getting them to reprocess questions that were answered incorrectly on the exam, and also checking source materials such as the text, lecture notes, and study notes used by that student for exam review. We examine how a student processes the stem of the question (i.e., the initial statement or question) and how this is related to subsequent handling of the various alternatives or possible answers that are offered in the question. We work together with each student to answer the following important question: "Why did you get questions wrong on this multiple-choice exam?" The answer usually indicates three problem areas: (1) preparation for the exam, (2) errors during exams, and (3) exam anxiety. Can you identify with any of these problems, and, if so, what do you need to do to develop more effective strategies for multiple-choice exams?

Preparation Problems

There are several problems that can arise when you are preparing for an exam:

- Too Little Time Spent Reviewing
- Studying from Incomplete or Inaccurate Information
- Comprehension Problems
- Ineffective Review Techniques
- Inflexible Learning Techniques

Too Little Time Spent Reviewing

Some students are so busy with other activities such as a job, sports, or social activities that studies really suffer. Usually this is because they do not realize how much study time is needed to succeed. However, poor test scores can lead a student to re-evaluate priorities and allot more time to review. Are you satisfied that you plan enough time to cover all of the material you need to know in an in-depth and flexible manner? Quality exam writing depends on both regular studying and effective review.

Studying from Incomplete or Inaccurate Information

Sometimes students spend many hours reviewing and learning from their notes. However, evaluation of their class notes typically reveals underlying problems due to poor attendance at class or to poor note-taking techniques (see Chapters 6 and 7). Poor notes mean a poor knowledge source for review. If you feel that your notes are an impediment to effective preparation for a test, compare yours with a class-mate's or check them with your instructor or counsellor. Good notes and good grades usually go together.

Comprehension Problems

Another problem may be that students have misunderstood some of the basic concepts, and poor exam results may be the first indication that they are on the wrong track. There are no easy answers to this problem. If comprehension problems are related to a few basic concepts, you may find that you are able to clear up the misconceptions by rereading your text and rethinking the problem through or by discussing the issues with someone who understands the material well. If the problem is bigger than that, perhaps due to lack of background knowledge in the field, you will have to make serious decisions about the amount of time that you will need to commit to that course. If the problem is severe, you may have to consider withdrawing from the course and taking remedial courses to focus on improving your background knowledge for that subject.

Ineffective Review Techniques

Many students review simply by reading and rereading their lecture notes and highlighted text over and over again. Effective review involves much more than this. Active learning strategies, such as paying attention to headings, summarizing key points, and reciting summaries using headings as cues, are needed. Self-testing and using old exams or your own generated questions are also essential for performing well on exams.

Inflexible Learning Techniques

A student may have memorized by rote instead of having a thorough understanding of key ideas. Consequently, they may only be able to answer questions if they match the material learned precisely. In high school, rote memory might have been enough to produce a good exam result, but post-secondary exams often call for more. Although some questions may only require straight recall, many more require application of information. The goal of the Good Strategy User is to learn information in a flexible way that makes it possible to be a creative problem-solver on the test. In particular, students who do poorly because of inflexible learning strategies may have problems with (1) handling concepts presented through new and different examples, (2) making inferences that go beyond the basic information, and (3) relating known concepts to others in a broader context.

Errors during Exams

In this situation, the student does know the content but does not process the question accurately in the exam. If you identify with the problem of making too many errors during the exam even when you have a good grasp of the course content, the following may provide possible explanations:

- *Anxiety* interferes with your thought processes, causing poor or confused thinking.
- *Lack of academic self-confidence* makes you doubt your own recall, especially if there seem to be a number of reasonable alternatives that could be the correct answer to the question.
- You *overthink*—read too much into—the question instead of answering the question that is asked. If it looks too easy, you may think that there is a trick to the question and that there must be something more to the question.
- You *do not manage time well* on the exam. Either you speed through the exam, worrying that you will run out of time and so do not leave enough time to read or think carefully, or you dwell too long on problem questions and run out of time to finish.
- You make *reading mistakes.*
- You may *lose track of the stem of the question* or initial statement and choose an alternative or one of the possible answers because "it seems reasonable" even though it does not match what the question is asking.

Step-by-Step Approach to Writing Multiple-Choice Exams

You will need to develop effective strategies for writing multiple-choice exams to minimize errors during exams. The following step-by-step approach to writing multiple-choice exams may help you to improve your performance. The steps include:

- Cover Up the Alternatives
- Read the Stem of the Question
- Process the Stem of the Question

- Predict a Possible Answer
- Check the Format of the Question
- Process Each of the Alternatives
- Identify the Correct Response
- Reread the Stem of the Question
- Eliminate Wrong Answers
- Guess

Let's take a look at each of these. (Sample multiple-choice questions following this section will help to clarify these steps.)

Cover Up the Alternatives

It is easy to fall into the trap of reading the entire question too quickly (i.e., the stem or initial statement and all of the alternatives or possible answers). Covering up the alternatives with a ruler or small blank index card as you read the question stem will ensure careful and thorough reading and allow you time to carefully consider what the question is asking. If you do not take this first step with care, you may find yourself in difficulty: first, you may skim over the stem of the question so quickly that you misread it; second, you may be overwhelmed by the sheer quantity of information in the entire question and begin to panic; third, many of the alternatives may be incorrect statements and may begin to interfere with your knowledge base, leading to confused recall.

Read the Stem of the Question

Now, read the stem of the question or initial statement quickly but carefully to get a general idea of what it is asking. If the stem is very short, you may be able to arrive at a complete understanding with this initial reading. However, if it is a longer question, you will need to process the question further to understand fully what it is asking.

Process the Stem of the Question

This is the crucial step of arriving at a precise and accurate understanding of the question.

- ☑ Underline key content words.
- ☑ Track for limiting terms such as always, only, and never.
- ☑ Rephrase (translate) the question into your own words.
- ☑ Activate your knowledge base for relevant information about that particular topic or question.

This is the step at which many of the in-exam errors originate. You need to take care in decoding the stem of the multiple-choice question. Ask yourself, "What is this question really asking?"

Predict a Possible Answer

You may be able to predict the answer to the question without reading any of the alternatives. This may be possible if the stem of the question is a complete question in itself and you have recalled appropriate information from your long-term memory. Even if the stem of the question is incomplete without the alternatives, ask yourself the question, "What do I remember about this concept?" If you can locate the original material on which the question is based in your long-term memory, you will trigger recall of associated details that can help you to answer the question.

This step is another major stumbling block in answering multiple-choice questions. Many students do not make use of the knowledge they have. There can be a tendency to believe that the correct answer will "hit you in the eye" as you look at the alternatives. This is not so; you need to recall very actively the relevant information.

Check the Format of the Question

Some questions have combination answers such as "a) and d)," "all of the above," or "none of the above." Before you evaluate these alternatives in depth, you need to know if combination answers are an option and, therefore, if you can respond positively to more than one of the alternatives.

Process Each of the Alternatives

Read each of the alternatives for meaning, not just to recognize familiar terms or phrases. Essentially, each alternative is a true/false statement, and, keeping the stem of the question clearly in mind, you need to make a response to each alternative:

- I think this is true.
- I think this is false.
- I'm not sure at this time.

When processing alternatives, there are some pitfalls for unwary students. Although exams vary from instructor to instructor, there are three common pitfalls:

1. **Familiar phrases from the course.** If you recognize rather than think through an answer, you may get caught out by a statement that was learned

as part of the course material but that does not answer the question that is being asked. That is, it is a true statement in itself but not a correct answer for the question.

2. **A fact from your general knowledge.** Instructors know some of the beliefs and facts that are likely to be part of your general knowledge, and they may present one of these statements as one of the alternatives.

3. **Jargon.** Sophisticated terms can tempt students. You may see a word or phrase in the question and think that because it sounds impressive, it must be correct. In some cases, instructors make up terms in multiple-choice questions, and these can trap the unwary student.

Identify the Correct Response

If you understand and have a good memory of course content and have processed the stem of the question and the alternatives fully and accurately, then the next step is to circle the correct response. If you are able to complete this step, you have completed the question. However, life is not always that simple, and you may need to reprocess the question using the following backup strategies.

Reread the Stem of the Question

If you were unable to identify the correct answer, the stem of the question may be where the problem lies. Even if not, it still makes sense to reread the stem of the question because there will have been a lot of processing since your initial reading.

Eliminate Wrong Answers

If you still have problems, try to reduce the number of alternatives by eliminating any that seem to be obviously incorrect.

Guess

Guessing is your last resort when all else fails, only to be used if there is no penalty for incorrect responses. Some marking systems deduct points for incorrect answers to discourage guessing. However, with all the processing that you have done so far, you will at least be making an educated guess rather than a stab in the dark.

Sample Multiple-Choice Questions

Each of the following questions has been selected to illustrate a specific point about different types of multiple-choice questions. Together, they demonstrate some of the types of questions you will encounter. One question might require straightforward recall of facts whereas another requires the use of a concept in a new setting. Multiple-choice questions vary a great deal, with each question dictating the depth of processing that you will need to answer it.

Remember that the way in which you identify main ideas and structure information as you learn is critical to success in multiple-choice exams. If you have been actively seeking main ideas as you learn, you will be better prepared for the exam. There are certain types of information for each subject that will be more commonly used to develop the exam questions. The following questions are from a psychology test.[10]

As you read these questions, use the step-by-step approach described in the previous section of this chapter. Begin by covering up the alternatives with a ruler or piece of paper and focus all of your attention on the stem of the question. Read it very carefully, looking for key words that affect the precise meaning of the question. This is essential to identifying the correct alternative or answer. The correct responses for the following questions are indicated by arrows.

1. If a wolf or dog rolls onto its back like a puppy, we are probably witnessing (**stem**)

   (**alternatives**)
   a) a threat display.
   b) a sexual display.
   c) ritualized combat.
→ d) an appeasement display.

This question is based on an example that illustrates and defines a key concept. The stem is a complete question in that the well-prepared student will be able to picture the animal behaviour described and, without uncovering the alternatives, recall where in the course that idea was introduced. The student will link together the example of behaviour (wolf or dog rolls on its back like a puppy) and its associated concept term (appeasement display). This recall question can be completed without reading through the alternatives. Always, with a complete stem, attempt to recall information from memory rather than depending on the alternatives to suggest possible answers.

---

[10] Thank you to Dr. Michael Atkinson for providing these questions.

2. Psychologists have often pointed to the similarity between territoriality in animals and personal space in humans. Available information suggests that personal space patterns in humans

   a) are instinctively determined in much the same way as in other animals.
→ b) are probably more a function of cultural and social factors than genetic determinants.
   c) are very similar across cultures and societies.
   d) are as predictable and automatic in humans as are territorial patterns in other animals.

The next question entails quite a bit more reading than the previous one. It involves a comparison of the related concepts of animal territoriality and human personal space. The well-prepared student should underline these concepts in the stem of the question. The question calls for an explanation of the behaviour associated with a need for personal space. The Good Strategy User who has been structuring information will have been identifying comparisons among concepts and explanations for key concepts such as this.

3. The "cupboard theory" holds that the mother–infant attachment is based primarily on fear of losing the individual that satisfies the infant's bodily needs. Which of the following observations, if true, would support such a theory?

   a) Even when well cared for, children display intense separation anxiety upon parting from the mother.
   b) Children often display attachments to individuals who have not been caregivers.
→ c) Infant monkeys form the strongest attachments to surrogate mothers that supply food, regardless of the physical characteristics of the surrogate.
   d) There appears to be no reliable difference in the quality of attachment of a human child to mother or father, no matter who is the primary caregiver.

The stem of this question states an exact definition of the cupboard theory and then asks students to select evidence that supports this particular theory. The well-prepared student will remember that this evidence was presented in class. However, for the less-than-well-prepared student, there are some real pitfalls written into the alternatives.

A good example of a pitfall is alternative a). It states that children display anxiety when they leave their mother. However, only some (not all, as implied in this alternative) children behave in this way. In addition, attachment theory, as defined in the stem, is about infants, while alternative a) refers to children — not exactly the same age group. Most importantly, though, attachment theory is about attachment, and alternative a) refers to separation anxiety — a different concept. It is important to keep the stem of the question clearly in mind and not to get trapped by statements such as alternative a) that seem to make sense but do not answer the question.

4. Suppose you lived in a culture in which people were ashamed and confused about eating rather than about sex. Such people might cover their faces and express shock at the sight of another person's lips and perhaps even limit their intake of food to unappetizing pellets consumed behind closed doors. In such a society, which of the following statements would be most likely to be uttered by a person displaying "projection," as defined by Freud?

   a) "As an artist, I am best known for my portrayals of pineapples and Swiss chard."
→ b) "I always notice Edith's devouring eyes."
   c) "Sure I subscribe to *Gourmet* magazine. Its articles on current events are excellent."
   d) "Yesterday I saw a truly disgusting sight — a huge roast turkey awash with rich brown gravy and cranberry sauce sitting beside a juicy apple pie. I tell you, it just about made me sick."
   e) "I was so angry with Dad last night that I called him a 'baked potato' to his face."

The stem of this question introduces Freud's concept of "projection" as it relates to sexual behaviour. This is the key concept, and the first step for the student is to define that term. With this definition in mind, the student can then evaluate the alternatives. This question employs analogies to test flexibility of knowledge. With this application question, the Good Strategy User has the ability to think beyond the information presented in class and texts.

Success with Multiple-Choice Exams

If you are well prepared going into a multiple-choice exam and have your anxiety reasonably under control, you have what it takes to do well on the exam. Some key strategies to remember are as follows:

- **Think positively.** You *do* know the information and the right answer is on the exam paper. All you need to do is match the two.
- **Take some deep breaths before you begin the exam.** Try to feel calm throughout your body. Let your muscles loosen and your body feel relaxed. Now you are ready to begin.
- **Plan your time.** Although there is a lot of work to do in the exam, there is also enough time in which to do it. However, an eye to the clock will help you to pace yourself. Try to maintain an unhurried but steady pace throughout.
- **Read carefully.** Precision is the key for multiple-choice questions. Circle key words and, in particular, evaluate exactly what the question is asking.
- **Recall information that is triggered by the stem of the question.** Do not depend on the alternatives to give you ideas about what it is you are looking for. Think, think, think!
- **Compare each alternative with the question.** If you lose track of what the question is asking, go back and read the stem over again. The stem and the correct alternative are like a lock and a key—they must match exactly if they are to work.
- **Learn from your mistakes.** Look over returned tests and exams, with the instructor if possible, to evaluate any errors you made.

ESSAY EXAMS

Writing an essay during an exam within a short time frame (usually less than an hour for each essay question), is very different from writing a term paper. The objective in the exam is to demonstrate that you have knowledge of the course material and can retrieve and organize information to answer the question that is posed. Thus, all students are using their own "data base" of memory, and the major skill required is the ability to answer the question succinctly, bearing in mind key priorities of the course content.

Although writing quality essays in exams is a difficult task for many students, it is unlikely that many students practise writing sample answers before they write the actual exam. Just as athletes need to train for an event, students need to practise for an exam. Practise writing essays as part of your review process, and you will be able to produce quality answers on the exam.

Common Problems with Essay Exams

Marks are frequently lost in essay exams due to the following problems. Do you identify with any of them?

- **You may not analyze the question carefully enough to decide what key issues are involved.** It is important that you understand and answer the question that is asked. A common error with essay exams is the "knowledge dump," where a student writes down as many facts as possible without focussing on the specific question.
- **Your essay may lack clear direction.** You need to inform your reader of how the essay will proceed, especially regarding the overall theme. It is important for you to provide the reader with some guiding information in the form of an overview or road map of the proposed order of subthemes.
- **Your essay may lack cohesion because the transitions from one section to the next are unclear or missing.** Attention to the integration of ideas, overall organization, and flow is essential if the essay is to be a success.
- **Your vocabulary may be too general.** Vocabulary that is specific to the discipline will give the ideas legitimacy. Appropriate use of academic language that precisely names the concepts involved is a clear indication that you really do know and understand the material.
- **Your essay may provide an overview of general concepts but lack examples.** You need to include specific examples to illustrate general statements that you make. It is the use of appropriate examples that really confirms your knowledge of a concept.

Each of the above problems stems more from a lack of thought about the way to present information rather than from a lack of knowledge. Within the time limits of the exam, this requires deliberate planning. Do not be influenced by those students who begin to write furiously as soon as the exam begins. Rather, take the time to survey the questions, make a reasoned choice, and plan a time frame for your answers so that you can allow sufficient time for each question.

Effective Strategies for Writing Essay Exams

1. **When you first read through the questions to decide which ones to answer, jot down a few words or phrases for each possible choice.** This will cue you as to how easy or difficult it is to recall relevant information for those specific questions.

2. **Review the comments you jotted down.** Use them to guide your final choice.

3. **If possible, begin with a question about which you feel confident.** Budget time to match marks, and spend more time on questions that are worth more marks. Be careful to answer the correct number of questions. Plan to spend a few minutes at the end of the exam to review and edit your answers.

4. **As you answer each question, plan a point-form answer.** It can consist of the following:

   • a statement of the main or controlling idea that will guide the whole essay (if this is appropriate to the question);

   • points about content to be considered in order (ideally, one to each paragraph or set of paragraphs); and

   • reference materials or names of important people and events.

   Generating point-form answers is something that you can practise with one or two friends before the exam. Think up essay topics as a group. Then each person can outline answers (say, four in an hour) and you can compare notes. This will consolidate your knowledge as well as raise the level of your skill in outlining exam answers.

5. **Write your essay in a standard format that includes an introduction, body, and conclusion.** (See Chapter 11, "Writing Essays.") Remember that someone has to read your work, so keep your handwriting as legible as possible. If there is a problem, write on every other line. Also, number your questions clearly in the margin. It can be very frustrating for the person grading the paper if it is unclear where the essays begin and end.

6. **As you write, periodically look back at the question to check that you are not straying off topic.** Maintaining focus is important to a successful answer.

7. **Finish on a positive note.** Even if you have doubts about having done justice to the topic, end the essay positively.

8. **Allow some time to check for spelling and legibility in your planning for a question.** When you have finished writing, allow time to read over your answer and check grammar. You may be rewarded by the grader if your exam is easy to read.

Common Types of Essay Questions

Three common types of essay questions are:

- Compare-and-Contrast Questions
- Analysis Questions
- Critical-Examination Questions

Compare-and-Contrast Questions

> COMPARE AND CONTRAST the most significant aspects of the role of the prime minister of Canada with the role of the president of the United States of America.

You will recognize "compare and contrast" as one of the most widely used phrases in essay exam questions. It requires you to discuss points of similarity and difference. A common problem is that students tend not to integrate their answers. Instead, they first write everything they know about the role of the prime minister, followed by everything they know about the role of the president. However, this is not acceptable as a good answer. A Good Strategy User compares each role on a point-by-point basis throughout the entire essay.

Analysis Questions

> ANALYZE THE SIGNIFICANCE of Canada's natural waterways to settlement patterns across the country. Use specific examples to illustrate any major impacts.

An analysis question calls for something beyond a simple descriptive inventory of waterways on Canada's geographic history. You will need to explore important controls on settlement such as accessibility and barriers, natural routes and their potential hinterlands, resources, trade, and politics. Include detailed examples.

Critical-Examination Questions

> CRITICALLY EXAMINE the contribution of Canada to the United Nations' peacekeeping operations from 1970 to the present day, with specific reference to the cost benefits.

Critical examination in an essay requires hard evidence for points that are made. You will need facts and will have to evaluate positive as well as negative aspects of Canada's participation in U.N. assignments.

Other Common Terms in Essay Questions

Besides the terms used in the three common types of essay questions, there is a whole range of vocabulary commonly used in essay exams. What is your understanding of the requirements of the following terms or action verbs?

assess _____

argue _____

describe _____

define _____

discuss _____

explain _____

evaluate _____

examine _____

illustrate _____

justify _____

predict _____

prove _____

Your Own Point-Form Answer

Generate a typical essay exam question. Use one of the commonly used terms from the previous two sections, and state the main or controlling idea that integrates the whole question. List at least six points or subthemes that you would expand on in your answer. Add any references, names, and events essential to a quality answer.

Essay Exam Question

_____

_____

_____

_____

Controlling Idea

_____

_____

_____

_____

Point-Form Outline

_____

_____

_____

_____

_____

_____

Important References/Names/Events

_____

_____

_____

_____

SHORT-ANSWER EXAMS

Some of the points made about writing essay exam questions also hold true for short-answer questions. For example, it is critical that you read the question carefully and answer exactly what is asked. It may be useful to make some quick notes before writing, but, often, because of the scope of the questions, you may be able to organize the answer in your head before beginning to write. This can be a real timesaver.

Before going into the exam, be very clear about the format required for the answer. Some instructors will accept point-form or even diagrammed answers. For example, in your earth science course, you may be asked to explain the mechanisms that have produced the Rockies, and a well-labelled diagram may be the most appropriate method to use for your explanation. In fact, in some instances, this is exactly what is required. However, in other cases, a carefully crafted answer is demanded, with careful, precise writing. Anything less will be unacceptable and will not score high marks even if full content is presented.

Finally, be very careful about making rigid assumptions about how much content is required in an answer. Some students believe, for example, that a short-answer question worth five marks should always consist of five statements. Always base your answer on what you think is a full and accurate response to the question regardless of how many sentences that entails. That is, always base your answer on content and not on a set number of points per mark.

PROBLEM-SOLVING EXAMS

The fourth type of format is the problem-solving exam, in which you must make logical decisions and calculations in subjects such as engineering, mathematics, physics, economics, business, etc. (See Chapter 8, "Problem Solving in Science and Engineering.") As with any exam format, it is necessary to be strategic. The following strategies are intended to help you to avoid common errors that students make when writing problem-solving exams:

- Write Down Important Formulas
- Pace Yourself
- Read Over All of the Problems First
- Start with the Easier Questions
- Write Neatly and One Step at a Time
- Monitor Mistakes That You Are Likely to Make

Write Down Important Formulas

Because of anxiety, you might forget some important formulas. It is a good idea to record a few of the most basic and important formulas before reading the exam questions. This is a good way of taking some of the load off short-term memory.

Pace Yourself

It is important to match time to marks. Many students get hung up on problems that are not worth very much. To avoid this, check the marks distribution at the start of the exam so that you can pace yourself accordingly.

Read Over All of the Problems First

This strategy has two important advantages over just jumping in to solve problems. First, you can decide which questions are easier for you, and second, you can do these while letting the difficult questions incubate in your brain. However, use this strategy only if you do not get even more nervous by reading over all the exam questions at once.

Start with the Easier Questions

Often, one type of problem will be easier for you than another. By reading over the exam (or a few of the initial questions) and then starting with one of these easier problems, you can build your confidence as you write the exam. Also, you are ensuring that you are doing problems that you know how to do before tackling ones that are more challenging.

Write Neatly and One Step at a Time

Many errors happen when work is not recorded systematically. Characters are misread, numbers miscalculated, and important signs are missed. Also, trying to combine several small steps into one very complex one can be a sure recipe for disaster.

Monitor Mistakes That You Are Likely to Make

You probably noticed mistakes that you made as you worked with problems throughout the term. If these were of a particular type, watch out for them on the exam. Hopefully, in your preparation, you will have monitored these kinds of problems and found ways to minimize your errors.

CASE-STUDY EXAMS

Case-study exams are most common in business courses, although they may also be found in a number of different disciplines such as nursing, social work, and others. Whether the case studies are to be completed in a short time period (say, 30 minutes) or are very extensive (one case study for a four-hour exam, for example), they have several characteristics in common.

- **Make sure that you have a sound understanding and knowledge of the relevant framework.** You have usually been taught a framework or set of considerations in class that you are expected to apply to each case. It may be useful to make a quick notation of the steps to cover in the case before you begin your analysis.
- **Be very clear about the goal of the case.** Where should it lead? It is common to have to make a judgement or recommendation at the conclusion of the case.
- **Set some time goals for the various parts of the case.** Even with four hours for a test, time can pass very quickly. You may have to push on through some of the steps with your eye on the clock if you are to finish the entire case in the allotted time.
- **Reading the case carefully is essential to a good result.** However, you will probably begin to process the case before you have finished reading it over. You may have to do both steps together and highlight key information during your initial reading. Key notes that you add to the margin can be a useful aid when you begin to write your summary for the case. Keep the case framework in mind as you highlight the main ideas.
- **Practise producing calculations before you go into the exam.** If you anticipate that there will be calculations such as balance sheets that need to be completed in the case study, review them ahead of time. This will ensure that you can generate the necessary structure in the exam in the minimum amount of time. Case studies usually require a recommendation

based on hard facts, and in a business case, these will usually be financial considerations.

- **Following the case framework, develop your case summary including all of the elements.** Use subheadings or distinctly separated paragraphs to clearly indicate the various elements. This will not only make the marker's job much easier, but it will demonstrate that you are aware of the case components.
- **Try to ensure that you stay on track and include only relevant information.** All of the points that you make should logically lead up to your conclusion or recommendation. With many case studies, marks are lost because too many digressions are made and unnecessary information given.
- **Pay careful attention to the quality and readability of your answer.** Before you write the actual exam, ask for feedback on your writing skills from your instructor. You can work through a sample case and give the instructor time to evaluate it carefully. You will then know if there are specific aspects of your writing that need improvement before the exam.

EXAM ANXIETY — GOOD OR BAD?

Many students report that they feel tense before an exam. For some students, these feelings of tension become magnified into a very real case of exam anxiety. The symptoms that accompany severe exam anxiety—stomach upsets, headaches, rapid heartbeat, or outright panic attacks—can be so debilitating that it can become difficult, or even impossible, to focus on the exam. Negative thoughts can interfere with concentration. Worries such as, "If only I had prepared better. This test is going to be so difficult. What if I mess up like last time?" can make it hard for any student to regain composure and continue with the exam.

Not all anxiety is negative. Being keyed up or "pumped up" can help you to focus the energy needed to achieve a high level of concentration. You may find that the exam is an exciting challenge—a time to put out that extra effort needed to do well. As a Good Strategy User, you will be able to generate positive energy from nervous anxiety and achieve peak performance while maintaining a moderate level of exam anxiety (see Figure 10.1).

Controlling Exam Anxiety

Worrying thoughts can be a serious problem during exams. The exam requires you to focus on one particular issue without being distracted by doubts about per-

FIGURE 10.1   RELATIONSHIP BETWEEN ANXIETY AND PERFORMANCE

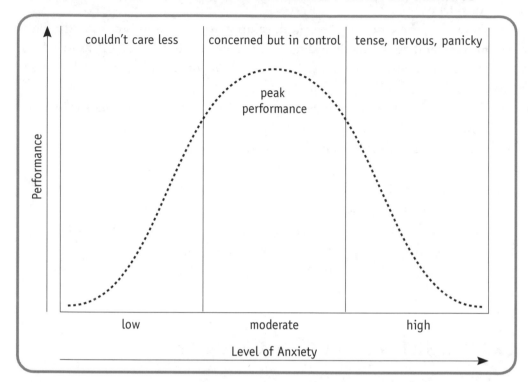

formance. As a student, you have to write many exams and, therefore, it is necessary to keep exams in perspective and to try to see them as steps on a ladder to success rather than as stumbling blocks.

Most students feel some natural anxiety and need to take a strategic approach to maintaining a positive attitude toward exams. It is best to plan ahead to control anxiety rather than to be surprised by losing concentration during an exam.

If your potential level of exam anxiety is very high, you might wish to check with a counsellor to ask about helpful techniques for controlling anxiety. Such techniques require time to learn and to practise—they are not a last-minute fix.

The following are strategies that you can use to control exam anxiety:

- Several Days before the Exam
- On the Day of the Exam
- At the Exam Itself

Several Days before the Exam

There are a number of different ways you can rehearse for an exam, as outlined in Chapter 9, "Preparing for Exams." These strategies stress the idea of rehearsing for the exam by working through typical questions using old exams, your own generated exam questions, study-guide questions, and other methods.

Find out exactly where the exam room is, what time the exam begins, and as much as possible about what to expect of the exam setting. Having a visual image of the size and layout of the exam room can help to reduce the number of unknown factors about the exam and can give you a better sense of control.

On the Day of the Exam

Be as well rested as possible. For most students, a good night's sleep is essential to effective performance. Pulling "All-nighters" or studying until the last moment is risky.

Get to the exam room in good time, but do not be so early that you have to wait around for a long time. Do not discuss content with other students, or you may begin to panic if you think they know more than you do.

Some students like to bring a lucky charm—a favourite sweater, pack of gum, picture of a best friend, or a talisman. Anything that allows you to feel more secure and confident can help to control exam anxiety.

At the Exam Itself

Take some deep breaths as you go into the exam room, choose your seat, and read through the instructions on the front cover of the exam.

Watch for signs of physical tension. Stretch some muscles if you feel that you are tense. Don't be shy—lots of people stretch legs, arms, and fingers in exams.

Use visual imagery to calm yourself down. Close your eyes and *see* yourself calmly writing the exam and doing really well.

Focus on positive thoughts rather than negative ones. Inner talk can give you a lot of personal control over anxiety. The following four cognitive strategies can help you control stress. If you can learn to use them when you are not under exam pressure, then it will be much easier to use them successfully when you are in an exam.

- **Keep your attention on the present.** Avoid thinking of past mistakes or future plans that might involve imagining negative consequences at a later date.

  What's involved here?
  What's the next step?

- **Concentrate on your own approach to answering questions.** Do not get too involved in watching other students in the exam or comparing their effort with your own. You have no control over other students, so it is a waste of time worrying about their performance.

What do I know about this topic?
What is this question asking?

- **Keep moving through the questions.** Try not to judge your own effort by criticizing the way you are handling the questions. Stay focussed and stay calm.

Now I will see how I can handle this next question.
How does the next one look?

- **Control your response to difficult exam items.** Avoid generalizing about the exam experience by entertaining negative thoughts about how poorly you are performing. Focus on what you do know rather than on what you do not know.

What did we learn about this in lectures?
The world will not fall apart if I get some questions wrong!

Don't be afraid to stop and take a break during an exam, especially if you regularly do that when you study.

Plan to give yourself a treat after the exam—have a party, meet a friend, watch TV, or rent a movie. This will give you something to look forward to as you write the exam.

WHAT SHOULD YOU DO?

Matthew turns the first page of the multiple-choice exam and begins to panic because the first question is from the chapter that he did not have time to read. What can Matthew do to stay calm?

_____

_____

_____

Faria is just about to begin the last essay question worth 20 percent of the exam. She looks up to check the time and finds that she only has five minutes left. What can Faria do in five minutes?

_____

_____

_____

Pari is about to write an essay question on the history of twentieth-century Canada. He knows so much about this topic that he doesn't know where to begin. What should Pari do?

_____

_____

_____

Paula is feeling tired. She studied really late last night for this exam, and she can hardly keep her eyes open. What can Paula do to improve her energy and concentration levels?

_____

_____

_____

TAKING CONTROL OF THE EXAM SITUATION

W HEN WRITING AN exam, you have an opportunity to show how much you know about the course material and to reap the benefits of all of your hard work with a good exam result. It is important that your grade reflects your knowledge of the course content and your ability to apply that knowledge to the examination questions. Because exams are a fact of student life, and you will find yourself going through the exam process on a regular basis, having a system that you can follow is one of the "secrets" to successful exam writing.

The strategies that you will apply when answering an exam question need to be matched with the type of question that you face. This chapter looked in considerable depth at strategies for the most common types of exam formats that you will likely encounter: multiple-choice, essay, short-answer, problem-solving, and case-study. Strategies were also suggested for another major exam-writing concern for some students—coping with anxiety. Although exam anxiety is not an easy problem to solve for all students, good planning before and during the exam can have a very positive impact on feelings of comfort and competency and, consequently, on the level of anxiety and performance.

Having explored the task of writing exams, the next two chapters look at other measures of student performance: "Writing Essays" and "Presenting Seminars." As you read these two chapters, think about the strategies that are shared in common by these three academic applications.

CHAPTER 11

Writing Essays

LEARNING OBJECTIVES

The purpose of this chapter is for you to:

→ Recognize the key features of a good essay.
→ Learn how to analyze the essay assignment.
→ Identify the structure of an essay.
→ Learn about the six stages required for writing an essay.
→ Identify the important features of paragraph structure.
→ Learn about self-help books on effective writing.

AN ESSAY ASSIGNMENT challenges you to explain your ideas on a topic in a clear and logical manner, presenting convincing ideas that help the reader acquire new insights. It is not an easy task to develop and synthesize new ideas in such a cohesive way. To write a good essay, you need to explore and research ideas, plan an outline, write a draft, and then revise and polish your final version.

Many students feel frustrated because they think that they waste time and energy trying to express their ideas in essays. They report that their final product does not reflect the time that they spent on research and writing. This chapter starts by identifying some hurdles to good essay writing. It then goes on to outline the steps that you, as a Good Strategy User, can use to express your personal ideas within the limits set up by your instructor. At each stage in the process of writing an essay, you have to recognize not only what is expected, but also what you can achieve within the available time frame.

MYTHS ABOUT ESSAYS

Some of students' frustration is a result of unrealistic ideas about the final goal. Here are some examples of student comments about essays:

- You have to think up something original that hasn't been said before.

It is seldom necessary to have original ideas. Rather, it is important to outline your point of view and present clear evidence to support it.

- You have to make reference to all the important works on the topic.

It is not necessary to consult every available source or even to find that definitive one. You may choose to use a few key items in your paper.

- The longer you research, the better your ideas will be.

The creation of ideas is important, but it may occur fairly quickly as the result of personal experience or initial survey reading. It is important to start writing sections of the paper as you go rather than leaving all the writing until you have done extensive reading.

The term "essay" is derived from the French verb "essayer"—to try. The essay is your attempt to express a reasoned argument given the specifications of your instructor. As you work on each essay, you will learn more about the essay-writing process. Being able to write well is one of the most important skills that you will acquire as an undergraduate student, but do not think that you have to begin by being the perfect writer. No essay is ever the last word or the best way of writing about a topic. If you can keep an open mind to the feedback you receive and approach each essay with a strategic plan, you can learn to write a convincing composition and gain confidence in your writing ability. First, let's look at the features of a good essay.

FEATURES OF A GOOD ESSAY

The following are features of a good essay:

- Cohesiveness
- Statement of Purpose (Thesis)
- Sources
- Organization
- Effective Language
- Correct Spelling and Grammar

Cohesiveness

A good essay presents information in a cohesive, logical, and reasoned way so that the reader can follow each idea from start to finish.

Statement of Purpose (Thesis)

In its introduction, a good essay has a statement of purpose or opinion, often described as the thesis. This thesis controls or focusses the way in which the main points of the essay are presented and developed. Therefore, every paragraph in an essay must relate directly to the chosen thesis. In the examples below, for instance, the essays associated with each of the two theses will be different although the general topic is the same:

- If society takes responsibility for controlling the pollution in our environment, it may be possible to stop the depletion of the ozone layer.
- The depletion of the ozone layer is the number one concern for society because, unless this problem can be solved, all other problems will be meaningless.

Sources

In many disciplines, it is enough to use only secondary sources such as survey texts or review articles in periodicals in a good essay. However, in some subjects, the use of primary sources—for example, government documents or literary works, such as plays—may also be required. Remember to credit all sources that contribute evidence to the argument.

Organization

A good essay presents the ideas that support the argument in a clear and organized sequence. You can refer to the next section, "Structure of an Essay," to remind you of the sequence that presents a clear argument. Be selective about the sources that you use so that they are consistent with your thesis and structure.

Effective Language

A good essay is more impressive if it uses vocabulary and sentence structure that present the ideas simply and clearly. Avoid jargon and pretentious language.

Correct Spelling and Grammar

A good essay must use correct spelling and grammar. It's a good idea to use spell check on your computer to make sure your essay is as accurate as possible.

ANALYZING THE ESSAY ASSIGNMENT

Every essay grows out of an assignment, and nearly every assignment (whether guided by an elaborate set of printed instructions, by a few brief suggestions from your instructor, or entirely by your own creation) requires you to answer certain questions. Sometimes, the assignment explicitly asks these necessary questions. Often, however, you are expected to "read between the lines" and decide for yourself what kind of essay the assignment requires. These ten questions can help you to plan a more realistic approach:[11]

1. **Formal Conditions:** What are the requirements of length, due date, documentation, etc.?
2. **Latitude:** How much freedom do you have to modify the terms of the assignment to choose your own way of answering these questions?
3. **Subject:** What, precisely, are you to write about?
4. **Purpose:** Why are you writing about this subject?
5. **Viewpoint:** What should be your stance as author?
6. **The Givens:** What information, assumptions, and materials do you and the reader begin with in common?
7. **Definitions:** Are there key words or concepts you must define?
8. **Organization:** What information, materials, ideas, subtopics, questions, and answers must stand out in your essay?
9. **Beginning and Ending:** Is there a particular point that you must start from and/or arrive at?
10. **Sources:** Which sources can (and should) you use?

When in doubt, ask your instructor before you start to write, but do not ask him or her to answer the questions that appear on this list. Instead, because you have thought about the problem, you can ask for help in deciding which of your alternative answers to the questions would most likely lead to a good essay. That way, you will be more likely to receive helpful answers than if you simply ask, "What are we supposed to do?"

STRUCTURE OF AN ESSAY

The structure of an essay can be broken down into the following three categories (see Figure 11.1):

---

[11] Adapted from materials by Joan McCurdy-Myers, Brock University.

- Introduction
- Body
- Conclusion

Introduction

The introduction provides your essay with direction and interest. The reader will want to know where he or she is going and what to expect. The introduction can provide preliminary information or background observations about the subject under discussion. It sets the tone for the paper. Generally, it should accomplish these four functions:

1. announce the subject;
2. interest the reader (by using apt illustrations, factors, or examples, or by explaining the significance of the subject);
3. state the thesis clearly and concisely; and
4. give a route map to the reader, mentioning the main topics or issues to be addressed.

Body

The body of the essay consists of paragraphs that develop the argument presented in the introduction. The first sentence of each paragraph should both introduce the paragraph and relate it to the other paragraphs in the essay. The transition sentences that join the paragraphs have three purposes:

1. to connect a paragraph with a previous one;
2. to point to the content of the new paragraph; and
3. to help to illustrate the thesis of the essay.

The evidence you present in the body of the essay should be arranged, where possible, in order of increasing importance with the strongest argument last. As a Good Strategy User, you should also make sure that you begin with a convincing point that will interest the reader in your perspective.

Conclusion

Several ways of ending an essay convey a sense of finality:

FIGURE 11.1 STRUCTURE OF AN ESSAY

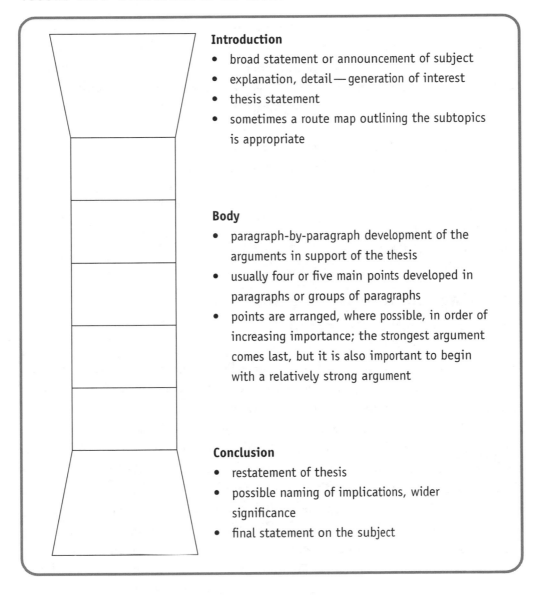

Introduction
- broad statement or announcement of subject
- explanation, detail—generation of interest
- thesis statement
- sometimes a route map outlining the subtopics is appropriate

Body
- paragraph-by-paragraph development of the arguments in support of the thesis
- usually four or five main points developed in paragraphs or groups of paragraphs
- points are arranged, where possible, in order of increasing importance; the strongest argument comes last, but it is also important to begin with a relatively strong argument

Conclusion
- restatement of thesis
- possible naming of implications, wider significance
- final statement on the subject

- summary of ideas with suggestions for further study;
- personal evaluation of the presented idea;
- appropriate quotation and comment about its significance; and
- extension of thesis into larger truth or universal consideration.

Naturally, you will not use all of the above methods in a single conclusion. Choose the method that seems appropriate to the subject of your paper. The basic principle is to restate the thesis and the strongest evidence and then end the paper gracefully without introducing new material.

STAGES OF ESSAY COMPOSITION

As a Good Strategy User, you can plan the process of writing your essay by following six stages. Setting up a timetable for the six stages will give you a more realistic idea of when to start the essay and when to move from one stage to the next. Keeping in mind how long each of the stages will take, count backwards from the date when you want to have the essay completed. The six stages are:

1. Choosing and Narrowing a Topic or Interpreting the Question
2. Gathering Information and Creating Ideas
3. Formulating a Point of View and Planning an Outline in Point Form
4. Writing a Draft
5. Editing the Draft
6. Polishing the Essay

Choosing and Narrowing a Topic or Interpreting the Question

If you have been given (or have chosen) a broad topic, you will need to narrow the scope so that your essay has a distinct focus. An unfocussed approach often results in gathering masses of information followed by the almost impossible task of trying to pull it all together into a coherent package. As you think about a topic, it is likely that you will begin with a broad global theme, but your goal at this stage is to narrow the focus gradually to a manageable scale. If you are researching an essay topic such as the destruction of forests, you could search the Web for information on specific types of forests (tropical, coniferous, etc.), for certain geographic areas (South America, East Asia), or look for data for a particular time frame (past fifteen years). In this way you can narrow your search to a set of information that you can discuss in a short essay. The following three titles show how the theme evolves from a very general topic to a much more specific topic:

General Topic:
- Rural to urban migration
- The impact on city schools of immigration from rural areas

Specific Topic:
- Social interaction in Pinewood High between the new and old residents of the school district

If you are given a statement or question to consider, you will have to analyze the issues. If the topic is "Computers have revolutionized society," you may ask, "What kind of computers and what does the term 'revolutionized society' mean?

Has the change extended to all of society or has it been limited to business, social, or economic concerns?"

Gathering Information and Creating Ideas

This is the stage when you check out different sources to find out what is available. Depending on the nature of your essay, you may find yourself collecting original materials such as interviews with local personalities, or you may spend time browsing the many different materials to be found in your academic or community libraries. You can retrieve many references through traditional indices or by using those on the Internet and CD-ROM, which provide extensive coverage on many different topics. If you are unsure about the best resource, a reference librarian can show you how to find those materials most relevant to your topic. You will not have time to read everything, so it will be necessary to make decisions about the most pertinent sources. Consider checking for:

- ☑ a combination of both old and new sources;
- ☑ a minimum number of sources (six to eight might be acceptable); and
- ☑ specific viewpoints that you may have explored in lectures or discussions.

*A **word of warning:*** It is common for students to spend too long in this information-gathering stage before making any decisions. Try to formulate a tentative, working thesis, to guide your selection of appropriate information. Being able to skim and scan a variety of sources can cut down on the time needed to research the topic. Skimming through paragraphs and making brief summaries, for example, will help you to focus on the information that illustrates and supports your thesis. If you input your summaries directly onto a computer at this stage, you will save time later during the writing stage.

Some texts will require thorough reading, and certain writing styles will need more careful tracking. As you read, it is a good idea to make notes on information useful to your topic such as interesting quotations. Some of the reading strategies in Chapter 7, "Learning from Textbooks," will help you to gather information efficiently.

Even at this early stage, writing is very important. Take time out from reading to formulate ideas on paper or on a computer. Writing and thinking are regarded by many instructors to be synonymous terms. Once you start to write your argument and to illustrate your points with pertinent evidence and references, you will start to generate additional ideas, and you may even change your mind about your point of view.

Recording Research Information on Your Computer

A computer is now an essential tool for storing and processing the evidence that you find for your essay and your own thoughts on the topic. An organized system of recording information on your computer can ease the challenge of essay writing:

- ☑ Create a bibliography by recording (in proper bibliographic form) each book or article that you locate. This reference will then be readily available to you any time. Adding the library call number will ensure easy access.
- ☑ Create a file for important ideas or interesting quotations that you will be able to refer to for any sources that you want to retain.
- ☑ Create a file to record your insights, personal summaries, and thoughts about the argument that you want to develop. This will provide you with a rich resource of materials from which to begin writing.

A note on plagiarism: Plagiarism occurs when students use ideas or words without indicating where they found them. This often results as much from poor record keeping as from deliberate misrepresentation. If you take care to identify your sources and to think about how you record the material that you want to include in your essay, you will be able to distinguish between your ideas and words and those of other sources, and to document these clearly.

Formulating a Point of View and Planning an Outline in Point Form

Many students hesitate to move on to this stage because it takes great effort to consider all the ideas collected, to come up with a specific point of view, and decide how your essay will be structured. It is much easier to keep reading and recording what others have written and hope that all the information will inspire an interesting outline.

However, do not underestimate how your ideas may change and new ones crop up once you start the process of assembling and writing out your thoughts. This phenomenon has been described as "thinking through writing." The Good Strategy User will allow time for this stage by making a conscious decision about when to begin writing an outline and acknowledging that it may not be possible to predict the final structure until a few ideas have been expressed. It may be helpful to refer to the "Structure of an Essay" section on pages 181 to 183 as you proceed to this phase.

With your outline on the computer, you can move ideas around without recopying them, and you will be able to check the flow of ideas and logic fairly quickly. However, as only one screen can be seen at a time, the overall structure may be more difficult to monitor unless you print out a copy from time to time. Looking at hard copy can also assist in making sure that your editing is meticulous. Make sure that you have a backup copy of each section of your essay, and be careful not to erase your working copy until you are sure that you have finished with it.

Once you have generated an outline in point form, leave it for a day or so before you write a first draft. When you return to it, you will benefit from having had time for your ideas to percolate before committing yourself to a particular point of view.

Writing a Draft

As you write your first draft, you need to keep your thesis in mind while writing the various subsections. Ideas will flow much more easily if you shelve your critical self while writing at this stage. You will have a chance to revise your composition and assess how convincing it sounds later, so it is not important now that each paragraph be complete as you collect your ideas.

Students sometimes report being "blocked" or unable to write at this stage. If this happens to you, try to focus on the ideas that you want to express and not think ahead to the final product. You might try talking into a tape recorder so that you have a rough idea of how you want to present the information that you think is important.

Editing the Draft

When you read through your draft, try to look for certain features that will guide the structure of your essay. Referring back to the original questions or topic, you could ask:

- Is your central thesis clearly stated?
- Does your essay answer the question that was posed?
- Does your argument stop or go off on a tangent?
- Are the main points arranged in a logical sequence?
- Do all the main points relate clearly to your thesis?
- Have you used all the main points gathered from your reading? If not, why not?
- Do you see any material that is not attached clearly to a main idea?

Try getting help from a neutral reader at this point. When you become very familiar with the topic, it is often hard to see the forest for the trees. Reading aloud to a friend is another way of checking for structure, organization, and clarity, and weeding out irrelevant material or unnecessary jargon. Check for linking words and/or sentences that indicate clearly when you move from one idea to another. These transitions are crucial to the smooth flow of your essay. (See Box 11.1 for examples of transitions.)

Make use of your computer to help you move through the draft of your essay and check for the relevance of each sentence and paragraph. You may find it difficult to discard ideas that you have collected carefully, but if they do not add to your argument, it is better to delete them from the essay. You are not usually rewarded for adding points that are not strictly relevant, and it is not good policy to have the reader searching for your train of thought.

One useful strategy is to create a new version of your essay (after saving the original) that omits points that do not seem relevant. Put it aside for a day or so, and then read it again to consider how each paragraph is helping to present your argument. You can also use this opportunity to check for grammar, structure, clarity, flow, and vocabulary. To assist you with your editing, further information on paragraphs and on the introduction and conclusion is outlined on pages 189 to 192.

Polishing the Essay

With your computer, you can be creative about the format and layout of your essay, the font you choose, the spacing of your headings, and the detail on your title page. You can also run a spell check, although the computer will not be able to identify errors that are real words. Take the opportunity to learn how to make

BOX 11.1 EXAMPLES OF TRANSITIONS

Furthermore: this leads to
Significantly: it is clear that
Nevertheless: the underlying factors are
Obviously: this allows for the conclusion that
And so: the following now seems obvious
Finally: all the evidence points to

full use of your computer to achieve a professional appearance for your essay. You will be able to hand in a much more impressive essay and save time in achieving correct referencing and bibliographical notation.

You may be required to use a style that conforms to a certain standard such as the MLA (Modern Language Association) or the APA (American Psychological Association). There are many manuals that cover these styles in detail. However, it is also useful to have available a recent journal article that is written in the style you need. You can follow it as a model, especially with regard to referencing and bibliography.

PARAGRAPH STRUCTURE[12]

What Is a Paragraph?

A paragraph is a group of sentences conveying a single unit of thought — that is, it presents and develops one idea only. The essay paragraph usually accomplishes these tasks:

- Makes an assertion (*topic sentence*).
- Explains the assertion (*clarification*).
- Provides evidence (details, *examples,* illustrations, or other types of proof).
- Comments on the *significance* of the evidence.

The assertion, or topic sentence, generally appears at the beginning of each paragraph. It tells the reader the exact topic with which that paragraph deals. The rest of the paragraph is devoted to explaining what that assertion means, by doing such things as defining the terms or clarifying the situation. It then defends the assertion by providing evidence through details, examples, illustrations, and other types of proof. Further, the writer may want to explain the significance of the evidence to the reader to be sure that the reader understands why these particular kinds of proof were chosen and can then judge the validity of the assertion. (See Figure 11.2 for a sample paragraph.)

---

[12] Adapted from materials by Maureen Bogdanovich.

FIGURE 11.2 SAMPLE PARAGRAPH

TOPIC SENTENCE:	What seems "natural," common, and harmless in the film *Psycho* actually becomes horrid and dangerous. That is, the central
Clarification:	features of the story—the innocent-looking young man, the quiet country setting, the opening detective story plot—all mislead the viewer to expect a tale about two bandit lovers on the run. Instead, the countryside becomes a burial plot, and the film records the twisted logic of a psychologically disturbed, lonesome
Examples:	young man. The money, for example, would ordinarily constitute the object of a vast search, but in *Psycho*, this money becomes unimportant to the examination of the complexities of a psychotic mind. The common act of taking a shower becomes a horror and a disaster for the young woman as well as
Significance:	for the robbery caper in which she is involved. Thus, one of Hitchcock's purposes is to bring the audience to sense the unexpected possibilities of disaster in our everyday routines.

Introductory Paragraph(s)

Introductions may extend to two or three paragraphs or even two or three pages, depending on the length of the essay. Most often, a paper under 5000 words long contains one or, at the most, two paragraphs for an introduction. The main structure of the introduction, no matter how long, begins with a broad view of the subject, develops the readers interest, and then narrows down to the point of the essay —the thesis statement. Generally speaking, keep your introduction as short as possible. (See Figure 11.3 for a sample of an introductory paragraph.)

Concluding Paragraph(s)

The concluding paragraph focusses the reader's attention on the purpose, thesis, and subject once again. The paragraph begins with a concluding statement, a restatement of the thesis, and then a general comment. It traces the implications or consequences of the idea outwardly to broader applications. It should accomplish the following functions:

FIGURE 11.3   SAMPLE INTRODUCTORY PARAGRAPH

TOPIC:	**Changing perceptions through time on masculinity and resultant behaviour changes.**
General Statement:	What has happened to the North American male? For a long time, he seemed utterly confident of his manhood, sure of his masculine role in society, easy and definite in his sense of sexual identity. The frontiersmen of James Fenimore Cooper, for
Development of Interest:	example, never had any concerns about masculinity. They were men, and it did not occur to them to think twice about it. But one begins to detect a new theme emerging in twentieth-
Thesis Statement:	century literature: the theme of the male hero increasingly questioning his roles in society. Today, society is more and more conscious of traditional maleness not as a fact but as a problem.
Route Map:	There are multiplying signs indeed that something drastic has happened to the way that the North American male is redefining who he is.

FIGURE 11.4   SAMPLE CONCLUDING PARAGRAPH

ORIGINAL THESIS:	**D.H. Lawrence's explicitly stated view of the place of women contrasts with his literary characterizations of Mrs. Morel and Lady Chatterly.**
Concluding Statement:	The characterizations of Mrs. Morel and Lady Chatterly, therefore, seem to contrast with Lawrence's directly stated opinions about the relationship between men and women.
Thesis Restatement:	Perhaps Lawrence unwittingly is revealing a subconscious dichotomy of belief. He appears to believe philosophically that women have a right to individuality but, in reality, prefers them to maintain a subordinate and inferior position. Maybe this goes a long way to explaining the difficulties Lawrence experienced in
General Comment:	his real-life relationships with women and his preoccupation with male–female relationships in his novels.

- remind the reader of the main subject and purpose;
- explore the greater implications and general significance of the subject; and
- convince the reader of the subject's value.

Proportion the length of the conclusion to fit the length of the whole essay. A short paper will require only one paragraph. In a long paper, however, you may wish to restate your thesis in one paragraph, fully summarize your arguments briefly in a second paragraph, and discuss the significance of your argument in a third. Keep your conclusion as short as possible, depending on the length of your paper. (See Figure 11.4 for a sample of a concluding paragraph.)

SELF-HELP BOOKS ON EFFECTIVE WRITING

There are many excellent books available to help you to develop better writing skills. Having some of them readily at hand so that you can check on any questions that you have can take some of the stress out of writing. The following is a selection that you should consider for your own library:

Buckley, J. (1998). *Fit to print: The Canadian student's guide to essay writing* (4th ed.). Toronto: Harcourt Brace.

Choy, P., Goldbart Clark, D., & McCormick, J.R. (1998). *Grammar and usage* (1st Cdn. ed.). Toronto: Harcourt Brace.

Flick, J., & Millward, C. (1999). *Handbook for writers.* Toronto: Harcourt Brace.

Gibaldi, J. (1995). *MLA handbook for writers of research papers* (4th ed.). New York: Modern Language Association of America.

Hodges, J.C., et. al. (1999). *Harbrace handbook for Canadians* (5th ed.). Toronto: Harcourt Brace.

Messenger, W.E., & de Brun, J. (1995). *The Canadian writers handbook* (3rd ed.). Scarborough, ON: Prentice Hall.

Northey, M.E. (1993). *Making sense* (3rd ed.). Toronto: Oxford University Press.

Norton, S., & Green, B. (1999). *Bare essentials, Form B* (4th ed.). Toronto: Harcourt Brace.

Norton, S., & Green, B. (1999). *Essay essentials with readings* (2nd ed.). Toronto: Harcourt Brace.

Roberts, J., Scarry, J., & Scarry, S. (1999). *The Canadian writer's workplace* (3rd ed.). Toronto: Harcourt Brace.

Robertson, H. (1995). *The research essay: A guide to essays and papers* (3rd ed.). Toronto: McGraw-Hill Ryerson.

Stewart, K., Kowler, M., & Bullock, C. (1997). *Essay writing for Canadian students* (4th ed.). Scarborough, ON: Prentice Hall.

Turabian, K.L. (1996). *A manual for writers of term papers, theses and dissertations* (6th ed.). Chicago: University of Chicago Press.

Wilson, W. (1995). *Print out: Using the computer to write.* Toronto: Harcourt Brace.

MEETING THE CHALLENGE

THIS CHAPTER BEGAN by acknowledging the fact that writing an essay can be a very challenging experience for students. However, an essay assignment also presents an opportunity for you to develop many of the essential skills that you will need in later years such as researching and selecting ideas, developing your own arguments, and expressing them clearly in writing. Given the volume of information that is available in our modern world, you will need these critical skills.

The main message of this chapter is to see the process of writing essays as a series of stages. By taking this approach, you can reduce what might seem to be an overwhelming task to a number of smaller and more manageable steps. In addition, by planning ahead and allotting a reasonable amount of time for each stage, you can control the essay-writing process so that you can stay on topic and achieve your goals. Keep this in mind as you read Chapter 12, since this writing process has much in common with preparing for seminars.

Presenting Seminars

LEARNING OBJECTIVES

The purpose of this chapter is for you to:

→ Learn about the three stages required for making a presentation.
→ Identify strategies for researching background information.
→ Learn alternative methods for structuring your presentation.
→ Identify useful techniques for making your oral presentation.
→ Appreciate how to create good visual aids.
→ Learn how to relax before and during your presentation.

MOST PEOPLE FEEL nervous about speaking in front of a group unless they have had extensive previous experience in public speaking. In fact, public speaking is many people's number one fear. As in the case of many other skills, it takes some practice to co-ordinate and make a presentation in an effective and relaxed way. If you have never given a seminar before or if you are feeling anxious about the event, then, as a Good Strategy User, you can benefit from reading this chapter.

This chapter starts by asking you to complete a survey about giving a seminar. It then outlines strategies to help you plan and prepare each of the three stages of your presentation: researching the information, structuring the ideas, and finally, presenting the information to an audience. If you have a plan to follow, you can produce a quality seminar and feel the satisfaction of making a positive impact on your audience.

HOW STUDENTS FEEL ABOUT PRESENTING SEMINARS

Students vary a lot in the way they feel about giving a seminar. For some, the experience is an exciting challenge and an opportunity to share ideas with peers. For others, there is more anxiety than excitement, often because students have so little practice in giving presentations. How do you react to some typical student comments?

	Yes	No
1. I will be too scared to speak.	___	___
2. My biggest problem is knowing what to talk about.	___	___
3. I gave a seminar before, and it was not too bad.	___	___
4. The instructor usually helps out if you get stuck.	___	___
5. I really don't know what to expect.	___	___
6. Everyone else in the class knows how it feels.	___	___
7. My hands always shake.	___	___
8. I'm always scared that I will go blank.	___	___
9. I don't think that it will be too bad.	___	___
10. I'm actually looking forward to it.	___	___
11. I'm scared that I will not be able to answer the questions.	___	___
12. I know that it will feel good when it is over.	___	___

Your comments?

13. _____

14. _____

15. _____

16. _____

17. _____

18. _____

RESEARCHING THE INFORMATION

Because researching a seminar topic is much like researching an essay, it will be useful at this point to reread pages 185 to 186 in Chapter 11, "Writing Essays." A Good Strategy User will pose key questions at this stage in the following areas and then do research to answer those questions:

- The Content
- The Topic
- The Research

The Content

- What is expected?
- Is the seminar to be a review of the literature, a report on original research, a presentation of your personal point of view, or some combination of these three?

The Topic

- Is there an assigned topic or is it your responsibility to generate an idea?
- Can you choose a topic of personal interest?
- What are reasonable limits to set for this topic?

- If you are reporting your own original work (such as experimental results), is it an interim update or a final report in which you present your overall conclusions?

The Research

- How many books, journal articles, or other sources of information do you need to use?
- How can you survey the information most efficiently?
- What is the best system for recording crucial information?
- Is there a theme or angle emerging in the topic that will be the focus of your presentation?
- Will the way in which you present the material affect your research? For example, do you expect to use a lot of illustrative material such as pictures or charts?

STRUCTURING THE IDEAS

Although structuring ideas for a seminar is similar in many ways to doing it for an essay, there are important differences. The reader of an essay can always glance back to previous sections if there is a problem with the flow of ideas, but a seminar audience cannot do that. Therefore, a good seminar will address the audience's need for clarity by providing a lot of cues about the sequence of topics so that the structure comes through clearly.

The Opening

Think of a way to get the attention of your audience at the outset. How you do this will depend on the type of seminar that you are presenting. Depending on the setting, you can begin with an anecdote, quotation, or question.

For all seminars, you should clearly tell your audience what the subject is and how it will be developed. It may be necessary for you to specify the goals that you wish to accomplish. Also, you may need to give some brief background to the main topic, but be careful not to detract from your major focus.

The Body

Seminars are most commonly organized around a small number of subthemes that fit together in a structure suitable for the topic. For example, begin with facts and description, followed by explanations and examples, and finish with significance and conclusions.

Clear transitions, such as from one subtheme to the next, will allow the listener to understand more easily. Because time can be very tight for many seminars, do not place your most important observations at the very end in case you have to finish in a hurry.

The Closing

The ending should be well planned to accomplish a particular goal. For example, if you have to persuade your audience to a particular point of view, then sum up with your strongest arguments. Do not give the audience any ammunition in terms of counter-arguments, but anticipate the reactions, and have some responses rehearsed.

It may be useful to review with the audience the original aim of your seminar and evaluate what you have achieved. If the seminar is to be followed by a question period, you need to anticipate some possible questions, and you might suggest some tentative ones to be explored.

PRESENTING THE INFORMATION

If the seminar is to go well, it is important that you plan and practise the delivery. Think of it as a performance, with you as the star. The following are crucial components in presenting the information:

- Rehearsals
- Location Check
- Your Notes
- Visual Aids
- Voice
- Body Language and Appearance
- Handling Questions

- Feedback
- Reward

Rehearsals

Practise the whole seminar aloud in a place where you will not be disturbed and/or in front of friends. Try not to rush through the material, and keep track of the amount of time it takes. You may need several run-throughs before you get the timing right. It is important to respect your audience by not going over your time limit. If the material is taking too long to present, cut out less important subtopics rather than trying to talk more quickly.

Over-rehearse the first few phrases so that they are fairly automatic and require less conscious thought. Prepare and practise your final statements. Imagine yourself in the seminar in a relaxed, positive frame of mind. In the hour before the presentation, exercise your lips and jaw so that they feel relaxed when you begin to speak.

Location Check

Check out the size, shape, and seating of the room where you will be presenting. Also, if necessary, know where the light switches and electrical outlets are located. Check equipment such as the lectern, computer, projector, screen, and tables, and watch out for things that you might trip over.

Try out your voice in the room and, if it is a very large room, talk to the back row. You will need to practise projecting your voice to gain control over your breathing. You do not want to appear breathless throughout the seminar.

Your Notes

What type of notes do you prefer—notepaper or cards? Even if they never use them, many people feel much more comfortable when they have a good set of notes. However, try to get away from total dependence on notes so that you can look at members of the audience and make them feel more relaxed and receptive to your presentation. Notes on a lectern are easier to read, and, because your head is positioned higher, you will be more audible to the audience.

Take care that your notes are not situated where they can get blown around in a breeze. Number the pages so that you can reorganize them quickly if, for any reason, they get out of order. Include large headings in your notes with space in between so that if you lose your place, you can find it again as quickly as possible.

Visual Aids

There are several choices of visual aids you can use to enhance your presentation:

- Overhead Transparencies
- Slides
- Video/Film
- Handouts

Overhead Transparencies

☑ Place only a few main ideas on each transparency. Most novices tend to overload the audience with masses of detail and lose the key points and relationships. Computer screen graphics produced by PowerPoint can help you to format consistent and effective visuals. Remember the K.I.S.S. mnemonic: Keep It Simple, Student!

☑ Use a font and size of type that is easy to read. Your computer software can help.

☑ Use colour and/or overlays to simplify complex information.

☑ Always give the audience time to read the basic information before adding any more information or analysis.

☑ Number your transparencies.

☑ Don't stand in front of the screen.

Slides

☑ Check the equipment to make sure that it is working properly and to ensure that all the slides are inserted correctly.

☑ Avoid going back to earlier slides. Have duplicates if necessary.

☑ Do not plunge the room into sudden darkness or snap the lights on without warning. It is very uncomfortable for the audience.

☑ Have a small flashlight on hand to check your notes.

Video/Film

☑ Check that your equipment is working properly.

☑ Avoid using really long segments that interrupt your presentation. Also, make sure that this illustrative material is really necessary and relevant to your topic.

Handouts

☑ Consider the function of handouts carefully. They can be distracting unless you distribute them at the right time. If the handout is to be used as an integral part of the presentation, the information should be kept short. Longer handouts are better kept until the end of the presentation, when more detailed information can be included.

Voice

On the way to the seminar, warm up your voice by humming a favourite tune. Voice projection can be improved with some easy exercises. For example, practise reciting a short rhyme with your teeth clenched tightly shut in order to exercise your lips.

> Mary had a little lamb, its fleece was white as snow,
> And everywhere that Mary went, the lamb was sure to go.

In the seminar, everyone must be able to hear your presentation, and so your pace should be slower and more deliberate than you would use in casual conversation. Aim for the back of the room, and look up at the audience. Pause at the end of phrases so that the listeners can follow your train of thought. Try to avoid a dry throat by sipping a glass of water, sucking a lozenge, or lightly biting the front of your tongue before you begin.

Body Language and Appearance

Try to be as natural as possible. Move around a little and, if you are overly conscious of your hands, hold something like a pen in your fingers. Wear something that is appropriate, tidy, and comfortable, avoiding elaborate decoration, jewellery, or noisy keys in your pockets.

Handling Questions

When someone asks a question, repeat or rephrase it so that everyone hears it. Take time to consider an answer since no one will expect an immediate response. Keep your answer short. If appropriate, give credit to the questioner with a comment such as, "That is a good question."

Do not try to answer questions if you do not know the answer. You can say, "I haven't considered that point yet," or "I am not sure that I have an immediate answer for that." However, if you anticipate possible questions ahead of time, you can have some responses ready. Also, have questions prepared for the audience.

Feedback

Ask friends who attend the seminar to give you both positive and negative feedback so that you get a balanced view. This will help you pinpoint those aspects of the content and delivery that you need to work on before giving your next seminar.

Reward

There is a lot of work and often a lot of nervous energy involved in presenting seminars. When you have finished the seminar, reward yourself for a job well done regardless of your view of your performance. This positive action will help you to feel better about presenting seminars in the future.

KEEPING CALM

Students who consciously plan their relaxation activities are often more able to handle academic stresses such as presenting seminars. When we asked students about how they cope with stress, they told us about many different strategies. Give each item on the following list a score to represent its use to you personally.

1 = very useful; 2 = sometimes useful; 3 = of little use

_____ Individual or team sports
_____ Walking
_____ Leisure-time reading
_____ Listening to music
_____ Playing a musical instrument
_____ Socializing with friends
_____ Watching TV
_____ Doing absolutely nothing
_____ Controlled breathing exercises

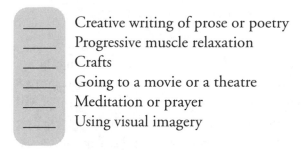

_____ Creative writing of prose or poetry
_____ Progressive muscle relaxation
_____ Crafts
_____ Going to a movie or a theatre
_____ Meditation or prayer
_____ Using visual imagery

An Exercise in Visual Imagery

Some people find that if they imagine themselves in a pleasant, alternative place, they can lessen the tension of a demanding situation. Read the following scenarios and choose one to develop further. Relax comfortably and imagine that you are in the situation. Try to explore the most relaxing aspects of such a scene. Revisit this scene whenever you are stressed.

> You are on a beach at the edge of a lovely lake with the water just washing over your feet. The water is cool and refreshing and there is a gentle breeze blowing. You can hear the birds calling as they fly low over the water.

> You are in a quiet pine forest with the trees stretching majestically upward. There is a faint scent of pine in the air and shafts of sunlight fall between the trees. The path on which you are walking is covered with soft, brown needles.

PUTTING IT ALL TOGETHER

THIS CHAPTER HAS emphasized that an effective seminar requires that you apply strategies to three important components of the seminar experience: research, structuring, and presenting to your audience. You will be more convincing as a presenter when you have spent time ensuring that you have organized the material in a thoughtful way. It is also important for you to consider ways in which to engage your listeners so that they are attentive to the information that you are presenting. It will take time and practice to become proficient in using the strategies discussed in this chapter. However, that time will be a valuable investment since your ability to communicate your ideas effectively will be advantageous on many future occasions in your career.

A STRATEGIC APPROACH TO academic tasks has been the unifying theme throughout *Learning for Success*. As you assume more and more responsibility for directing your own learning, the process of your learning will become as important to you as the academic content you are studying. Having read this book, you now have the model of the Good Strategy User to guide you as you plan strategies for your own self-management as a learner, as you explore the most efficient and effective ways to think about information, and as you apply your knowledge to the typical testing situations that students face. As a Good Strategy User, you can experience the academic success that you have worked hard to achieve.

ACKNOWLEDGEMENTS

We would like to acknowledge the contribution of the many students and colleagues who have shared their experiences with us and have provided support and encouragement for *Learning for Success*. We also appreciate greatly the continuing support of many people at Harcourt Brace & Company, Canada. Last but not least, we thank our immediate family members: Michael, Paul, Michele, and John Fleet; Michael, Penny, Kate, and Anne Goodchild; and Victoria and Alexandra Zajchowski. Without the interest and support of many people, this project would not have been possible.

Joan Fleet
Fiona Goodchild
Richard Zajchowski

Photo Credits

Dick Hemingway: pp. v, vi, vii (top), viii (bottom), ix, 1, 3, 13, 15, 42, 57, 78
First Light: (Tom Stewart) pp. 59, 135
Image Bank: (Michael Melford) p. 151, (Elaine Sulle) p. 24
Masterfile: (Michael Krasowitz/FPG) p. 93
Tony Stone Images: (John Brooks) p. 177, (Loren Santow) p. 114,
(Ian Shaw) pp. vii (bottom), viii (top), 149, 194

Index